T0355564

BOOKS BY *Grace Schulman*

POETRY
The Broken String
Days of Wonder: New and Selected Poems
The Paintings of Our Lives
For That Day Only
Hemispheres
Burn Down the Icons

PROSE AND CRITICISM
First Loves and Other Adventures
Marianne Moore: The Poetry of Engagement

TRANSLATION
At the Stone of Losses: Poems by T. Carmi
Songs of Cifar (with Ann McCarthy de Zavala)
   by Pablo Antonio Cuadra

EDITIONS
The Poems of Marianne Moore
Ezra Pound

First Loves and Other Adventures

Grace Schulman

First Loves and Other Adventures

THE UNIVERSITY OF MICHIGAN PRESS
Ann Arbor

A CIP catalog record for this book is available from the British Library.

Library of Congress Cataloging-in-Publication Data

Schulman, Grace.
First loves and other adventures / Grace Schulman.
    p. cm. — (Poets on poetry)
    ISBN 978-0-472-07087-9 (cloth : acid-free paper) —
ISBN 978-0-472-05087-1 (pbk. : acid-free paper)
    1. Schulman, Grace.   2. Books and reading.   3. Authorship.
I. Title.
PS3569.C538F57   2009
814'.54—dc21   2009033064

For Harold Bloom,
reader of masters
and master of reading.

Contents

Contents

Introduction

The writer's life begins with the passion for reading a book. There is the sense of a dangerous journey, destination unknown. Embark and you will hear a voice that speaks to one reader as it addresses all readers. Where that passion derives, though, is not in the book at hand, but in the emergent self, where, according to Emerson, all things start.

These essays are of two kinds: first, about becoming a writer; second, about some of the books I love. One of the pieces in the first group is about my aunt, Helen, who leaped or was shot from a tower in Warsaw, her act inspiring others, her courage releasing my own voice. Another turns on a childhood memory of my father reading to me in Polish, a language I did not know, the sounds leading me to lines by W. H. Auden, who had stirred to the same poems.

To labor in the art of poetry is to consider other arts and disciplines as well as other literary genres. Two encounters are with Genesis and Song of Songs, in the King James Bible. Thoughts about poetry and science were set in motion by two books with strikingly similar imagery, Muriel Rukeyser's *The Life of Poetry* and Lewis Thomas's *The Lives of a Cell.*

Most of the essays here have been published in journals. Some are new, others have been revised and expanded. For example, May Swenson's queries into the heart of things assumed new meaning when I found an early manuscript of her poem, "Question," and I amended my thoughts accordingly. A prose piece on T. S. Eliot's collaboration with E. McKnight Kauffer, the designer of his Ariel editions, was expanded to consider the poet's vision of renewal.

I've included an account of how Sylvia Plath's 1959 visit to Yaddo yields clues that illuminate her poetry's images. Two other essays are of poetry as a saving force in contemporary life: Octavio Paz persuades us that poetry can rebuild society; Karl Shapiro brings us a new awareness of the "unnumbered lives, unnumbered graves" in World War II. I have included thoughts about Léonie Adams, whose genius is largely unrecognized, and about Stephen Sondheim, whose genius is recognized, but only as a lyricist. My conviction is that he is a poet and a fine one if he is regarded as heir to a dramatic lyric tradition.

One of the new essays treats Marianne Moore's use of the sequence form as a way of seeing beyond surface appearances. Another is a portrait of Richard Yates, a novelist whose lessons on reading and writing are invaluable to poets as well as to prose writers.

I wish to thank the editors of journals and books in which some of these essays first appeared, sometimes in embryonic form, their attributions given on individual headings. For encouragement and help, I'm indebted to Carol Muske-Dukes, Susan Shapiro, Michael Collier, Richard Howard, Marianne Craig "Bee" Moore, Zan Knudson, Karl Kirchwey, Mary Ann Caws, Gerald Stern, Marilyn Hacker, Annie Finch, Alfred Corn, Simon Rendall, Philip Schultz, and Yerra Sugarman. Ellen Bauerle, Alexa Ducsay, and Marcia LaBrenz were among my angels at the Press. I'm beholden to PSC-CUNY for a research grant that facilitated the work, and to Simone Kearney, my research assistant, who was indispensable in the preparation of this book. Inspiration came from my students at Baruch College, and from my friend and colleague, Agha Shahid Ali. Shahid, in his ongoing quest for reading, often quoted Jean Cocteau, who when asked what single thing he would carry away from a fire, answered "the fire."

I'm especially grateful to Harold Bloom, who enabled me to see that great books can help us live our lives. Above all, I thank my husband, Jerome Schulman, for his patience and wisdom.

Helen

In my childhood, there was no actual peril. I wore starched pinafores, ate turkey with an attentive family, and lived in New York only a walk from the Hayden Planetarium. On Saturdays, I was taken to Carnegie Hall. I went to good schools and expected to go to college. All the same, I sensed that some demon waited to destroy us all.

Even before "the war," as we called World War II, I was acquainted with that fear. On the Knabe piano in the West Eighty-sixth Street apartment of my childhood, there were portraits of people who experienced danger and people who imagined it. Often I watched them move and invented stories about them, for my mother arranged and rearranged our family photographs in silver rectangles, in golden ovals with velvet mattes, and in brass squares with scroll-shaped edges. She collected those frames from junk shops on Third Avenue, and although she let them darken and develop shadowy crevices, she changed their locations the way a director places his actors, giving them life.

Some of the pictures were of our American relatives. Others were of living kin I had not met, such as my paternal grandparents. Having left Poland with two of their daughters in the 1930s, they raised vegetables and some livestock in Israel, and already possessed the grained, lizardlike skin of farmers with years of exposure to the sun and the wind.

Another photograph was of the family just before the move to Israel, when my grandparents and three daughters traveled from Warsaw to Danzig, then an autonomous city on the Baltic

This essay first appeared in *Testimony: Contemporary Writers Make the Holocaust Personal,* edited by David Rosenberg (New York: Random House, Times Books, 1989).

seacoast, to meet their son and his new wife. My father had asked that they assemble there rather than in Warsaw, which held memories of poverty and oppression. My parents had sailed for that encounter, returning from Berlin on the SS *Bremen's* last passenger voyage to America.

In that portrait, family members exaggerated their roles, as though they were the beams of a crumbling structure. My father stood stiffly with my mother, who blended adventurously with the foreigners despite the leggy stance, the knitted suit, and cloche hat of a New Yorker with generations of American Jews behind her. My father was emulating his father, who sat erect and stern next to his smiling wife. Posing as authoritative, my grandfather was actually a reticent man given to a lifetime of study in the house. With them were two pretty aunts wearing man-tailored suits and neckties.

Still another photograph, an enlargement in an ivory frame, was of Helen, one of the aunts who, in the group picture, stood looking off to one side. "She was a lovely sprite," my mother said of her sister-in-law. "That time in Danzig, she had just earned her degree in medicine and wanted to cut loose. She sent postcards to all of her boyfriends (there were quite a few), and she scrawled, 'I love you very much' on every one."

To me, Helen's face was not simply carefree. Her gaze was soft and yet insistent; her smile was compassionate but icy. Her prim black dress was edged with maidenly lace and unexpectedly cut low. Like women I had seen in a movie of *Ivan the Terrible*, she had high cheekbones and wide-set eyes that were trusting and, at the same time, sharply inquisitive. Then as now. I have noticed that she looks older than her sisters and brother, and yet more vulnerable. Unlike them, she seems careless of her appearance, as though any risk is worth taking that will forgo surface vanities for deeper truths.

Often I glanced at her mouth, then turned away in terror. She seemed to be straining to speak to me angrily of hardship and pain, and of a fierce price she paid to be alive even then, as a young woman in Poland.

I was drawn to Helen even before I learned after the war that Helen had died in the Warsaw ghetto uprising in 1943. Her picture remained where it was and often my parents would pause to look at her. During that time, I must have stared at her frequently, for the piano was central to my family of musicians manqués. We all played, though woodenly, and while waiting for some heavenly sign that would improve my scales I would wander to the bookshelves, where I heard my real music in volumes of poetry and, returning to the piano, fasten my eyes, somewhat desperately, on those photos. I remember Helen's name (actually Helena, but my parents Anglicized it), although I have forgotten many other names of the time. For me there were groups, such as children, classmates, relatives, workers, Democrats, Communists. Then there were individuals: Deborah, Persephone, Antigone, Helen.

Helen was the second oldest of three boys and three girls born to Benjamin and Mary Waldman of Łódź, a city south of Warsaw, in Poland. When their home was destroyed in an anti-Semitic demonstration, my grandparents fled with three of the children to Włocławek, while the oldest boy, Jan, along with Helen and my father, Bernard, remained in Łódź to study. Jan died of a chest infection, having suffered poor health from his pneumonia in the Polish army early in the century. He had fought in a skirmish when the Russians entered Poland in an effort to dominate that country. After Jan's death, Helen returned to her parents' home in Włocławek. Driven by fear, by the wish to be educated and the need to survive, my father left Poland for Germany and then England, where he studied law at the University of London before emigrating to America, then finished school at City College in New York. After brief careers as an actor and as a lawyer, he started a small advertising agency that he managed for the rest of his long life. A younger brother, Solomon, had joined my father here, and the sisters remained with their parents in Poland.

My grandmother, who opened a shop in Włocławek, sent Helen to medical school in Warsaw. Years later, when her brothers spoke of how she bandaged cuts and massaged her mother's shoulder, I resented their condescension. I assumed that she earned her education by meriting higher grades than they. Her gentleness, I felt, was a myth: I envisioned her stealing apples from a shopkeeper who had ridiculed her for wearing drab clothes. I imagined that she was annoyed with her brothers and her colleagues for valuing the woman doctor only for her role as nurturer. I do know that she was furious when professors called her "that one," asked her religion on examinations, and forced her to stand in back of an amphitheater during lectures even when there were empty seats.

My father told me that Helen had introduced him and his brother Jan to the poems of Adam Mickiewicz. He tried to teach me Polish when I was a child and, believing he had succeeded, recited that poet's ballad of love's triumph over reason. He, Jan, and Helen had shared German poems as well, notably Heine's and Goethe's, the acquisition of European languages being simpler for that border-inhabiting Jew than for his linguistically inept daughter. Although he was reluctant to speak of his past for fear of igniting anguish, he retained the poems all of his life and declaimed them in vehement tones. As for me, then as now my ear has been tuned to English poetry. Nevertheless, those mysterious Polish words were, for me, the fire of language.

I imagined Helen speaking the poems my father had intoned, in that bellowing utterance close to song. I thought of her narrowing her eyes and trying to concentrate on the poems, trying to focus on her studies, trying to ignore the inequalities that were imposed on her. Later I realized she struggled through winters of chest colds and of hunger, her drafty room less of a trial than loneliness. Her worst pain, I know now, was in being deprived of a name and a voice by professors who taunted her and who made silence her price for attending school. At the time, though, before the war, I suppose I scanned Helen's photograph without comprehending why I sensed her resentment. Next to her on the piano was a picture of me in a sailor's middy, writing alphabet letters in a notebook. We had the same eyes, the same cheekbones. I saw in her a darker version of myself.

Early in the 1930s, my parents learned that the Waldmans had emigrated to Israel. One of the sisters, Beta, joined a kibbutz, and the others settled nearby. Only Helen, who married Władek Gold, did not leave. She and her husband, both pediatricians, remained in Warsaw with their medical practices.

"Helen felt that she was needed in Warsaw," my mother said in around 1940, when I searched Helen's picture to fathom her decision. At the time Helen was lost to us, but her fate was still uncertain. "Helena Waldman-Gold," my mother mused. "That's what she called herself. She kept her maiden name by hyphenating it. I'm certain it was her wish to stay, and not anything Władek asked her to do. There were hundreds of children in that sector, and only a few doctors. She thought the Nazis would not dare touch them in that position."

"It's complicated," my mother continued, as though trying to assure herself of some hidden wisdom in Helen's decision. "She was afraid, yes, but she felt she had as much right to her country as we do to ours. Her patients trusted her, and she wanted to help them with her skills. She thought it would be safe for her and Władek, and perhaps she was right. Perhaps they are still alive."

My father had a different view of Helen's choice. "Headstrong," he said. "If only she had listened. She never listened. So, go on. Be a hero." He glanced at me as he spoke, and I knew what he meant. All Jews must be cautious in order to survive, but Jewish women must bend to authority. It would have been better for Helen to believe her father's stern demeanor in the photograph rather than in his actual meekness. She should have followed her husband, who, my father assumed, did not wish to remain in Warsaw.

I remember my father's remonstrance because it was the last time he discussed Helen's behavior. In the years that followed, he became depressed when he did things other than work. There were times when he recited no poems and hardly spoke at all, for language only heightened his terror. Occasionally he would break the silence to utter undue concern about the warmth of my clothes or the safety of the local skating rink. Sometimes he would look at my hair, which I wore in long braids as she had. Sometimes he would call me by her name.

My father's silences fell beyond the far reaches of my memory, and I can only reconstruct what I cannot recall of the Hitler period. For us in America it was a time of distortion, when our ignorant suspicion gave rise to luminous horror fantasies. In that mysterious atmosphere, the evasion of hope was deemed more dangerous than denial, because more cowardly. Before the war the news of persecution was gradual and there was reason to think that some Jews might be spared. After 1941 we woke to the mass annihilation of millions of European Jews to find that our trust was gone and our fantasies were feeble imitations of the Nazi atrocities. By 1942 the newspapers were filled with rumors of death camps and mass graves and forced marches in the name of a proposed Final Solution for the Jewish populace.

In retrospect, the adults' illusions during the early and middle 1930s seem understandable in the light of scant facts, the perception that anti-Semitic acts were not born in the decade, and the climate of faith in America and in the world. In the family photograph taken in Danzig, my parents' faces shone with an optimism I have never understood but have always known to be genuine. Once my mother recalled, self-ironically, that when she and my father stopped in Berlin en route to New York, "they were beginning to play those German songs, and men in uniform wore armbands with swastikas. I asked your father what those swastikas were, and he said, 'I don't know. Perhaps they are meant to identify the blind.'"

Whether or not she recounted that incident in my childhood I do not know, but I'm certain it was central to my concept of the Nazis. Often I dreamed of blind uniformed men on blind horses leading a blind population, naked and on foot, to their death.

Reality was no less surreal, or so it seems to me now. In 1933, with Hitler's rise to power, my family knew the Nazis had burned books by Jews and non-Jews and had boycotted Jewish stores. In 1938, they were aware of Kristallnacht, "the night of broken glass," in Germany, when Jews were beaten and their store windows were smashed. They knew of the deportations of Jews in Germany and of the harassment of Jews in Poland even before the Nazi invasion of 1939. Helen's letters stopped coming at about that time, and my father enlisted Jewish organizations to find her. Recently I discovered a radiogram from Poland dated December 15, 1939, addressed to my father and signed "Kuba Szejnberg," bearing the legend, "Delayed in USSR." The message read, "WALDMANOWNA LIVES ADDRESS UNKNOWN ANSWER QUICKEST." It was his last futile hope.

Memory began to assume sequential form for me during the

war years, when refugees from France and Germany came to live in my neighborhood, struggling to put down roots in America. Many of the settlers were women, and I inferred that *refugee,* which rhymed with *flee,* meant *woman in flight,* or the woman who must run and hide before her rebellious demon stirred her to express disobedience to the man in her household who posed as the stern father image, such as the one in the Danzig photograph. They had to leave, I thought, before the blue numbers appeared, those marks that had been tattooed painfully on their arms in invisible ink to tell the compliant from the troublesome.

Once I asked my friend Joan Kenny, a gentile, if she and her mother had to hide until the war was over. I knew that her parents were divorced and that her father, who lived in London, might not see Joan until the war was over.

"Hide? No. We are safe here in America. That's what Mr. Wolf said today. Does your family have faith in America?" I dared not ask my stricken father. I would not ask my mother, who tried to shield him by diminishing the tragedy.

Despite the religious difference, I made little distinction between Joan's situation and mine, an impulse to which I may have been bred. My family detested discrimination and denied the importance of boundaries between people. By and large, they chose camps and schools that ignored those divisions as well. They believed that persecution of any minority group was a threat to any other, and maintained that conviction when events might have pressed for a partisan stance.

They persisted in that view even though they knew an anti-Semitism that I had not yet encountered. My father remembered it from the Poland he left. After that, he experienced university prejudice in London. Then his best friend, an anthropologist, had been refused a teaching position there. My father would throw down his newspaper when he read vitriolic speeches by Father Coughlin and his face would darken when he heard radio reports of demonstrations by American Isolationists who blamed the Jews for America's having to enter the war. From polite gentiles they heard so many insults to Jews, ranging from subtle to gross, that they prefaced all such conversations by identifying their religion. "I don't like the *galut* Jew," my father said, using a word that meant "exile." "The *galut* Jew tries to forget his heritage. That's a terrible mistake."

My mother's family believed that a Jewish state would be gifted culturally and with equality. Her father, David Freiberger, was a lawyer who, as president of a Brooklyn yeshiva, had run a series of poetry readings by Hebrew writers, including Chaim Nachman Bialik, who visited in the 1920s. On a wall over Grandfather's desk hung a framed letter from Supreme Court Justice Brandeis thanking him for his help in founding the village of Herzlia, which was then in Palestine. His wedding trip had been to Palestine and when he died my parents spared Esther, his aged mother, by telling her he had gone to visit a kibbutz in Israel. For them the cure for prejudice against blacks, women, Jews, and other minorities was to be found in the kibbutz, which promised justice for all.

It was only after the war, though, that Israel held that trust, both because of the formation of the state and the end of gloom. Our synagogue helped in that regard, and also assured me of women's privilege. It bore the unwieldy name of the Society for the Advancement of Judaism. At my bat mitzvah, Rabbi Ira Eisenstein asserted that freedom for one minority was freedom for all and that Israel would be the place for the new equality. He spoke of the Jewish heritage as a gift and of womanhood as a blessing. "Seize the day and follow your heritage," he told me from the pulpit. "Women are natural leaders, and wise women leaders are common in Jewish history. Besides, no boy could have sung your haftorah as well as you did."

That confidence, however, came years after we learned the terrible answers to what had occurred in Europe. During the war, only patriotic faith in our Allies would deliver us from evil. The war's despair taught my parents that restraint was the price paid for American sanctuary. Subdued as he was, my father admired Kafka and Rilke, especially in passages of anguish. Nevertheless, he found that silent resignation was his only armor for protecting his coherence as an individual in a world where protest had lost its meaning and where decency and even life depended on preserving one's own free square yard. Silence was essential in dealing with the Holocaust that haunted our home without ever entering it.

For some time after they knew of Helen's death, my parents collected books with photographs of Nazi desecration.* They kept them on the shelves along with books they thought unsuitable for a young girl, hoping to avoid censorship while permitting me *not* to read books about human devastation. The records of horror had *The Black Book* in their titles and were published between 1942 and 1946. One that I remember vividly was *The Black Book: The Nazi Crime Against the Jewish People.* The bindings were black, as their names implied, and flimsy; the pages were brittle and yellow even when they were new.

Apparently my parents had no qualms about my reading Joyce's *Ulysses* and Lawrence's *Lady Chatterley's Lover,* or even books by Henry Miller and Frank Harris, all within easy reach. On the Black Books' shelves were less literary erotic books, but my mother didn't stir when I opened them. It was only when I looked at the Black Books that she seemed worried and told me once that I needn't feel I had to read them. It was then I associated the Holocaust with pornography.

The last of the books was filled with black-and-white photographs. I pored over the pictures: There were prisoners digging graves for other prisoners who were led to the pits, stripped, their hands covering their private parts. On mounds there were chains of naked, dead, emaciated bodies, bodies in hell, bodies distorted, tortured, misshapen. I thought of a painting I had seen of *The Last Judgment* by Jan van Eyck, at the Metropolitan Museum of Art nearby. The painting had disturbed me, and when I studied the photographs I knew why. As I stared at the camp victims, the corpses lost their distinctions and became one corpse, in one solid mass of horror. Only the faces were diversified, and Helen's face, in the picture I knew of her, was superimposed on each one. Gradually, as on film in developing solution, each face became Helen's. Then each face became mine.

---

* Three of the books referred to here are *The Black Book of Poland* (New York: Putnam, 1942); *The Black Book of Polish Jewry: An Account of the Martyrdom of Polish Jews under the Nazi Occupation,* edited by Jacob Apenszlak, Jacob Kenner, and Isaac Lewin (New York: American Federation of Polish Jews, 1943); *The Black Book: The Nazi Crime Against the Jewish People* (New York: The Jewish Black Book Committee, 1946).

When the Allied victory ended the nightmare image of the Holocaust, it also made that picture a concrete reality. A letter came from Beta, one of the aunts in Israel, who had news of Helen from a refugee organization. Still unable to speak of Helen, my father did not show the letter at home but did give it to Rabbi Eisenstein, who published it in the synagogue newsletter. Helen had moved to the Warsaw ghetto, where her husband had died in a typhoid epidemic. She believed she would be deported to a concentration camp, for there were rumors of the forthcoming ghetto liquidation. A survivor of Auschwitz, then in Israel, reported that he had known Helen in the ghetto. He said that he had seen her climb the tower of a municipal building, run to the ledge, and pull down the Polish flag from its staff. With a strength that seemed to startle her, she ripped the flag into shreds. Then she stood for a while, holding the red cloth and smiling before she was shot down by a Nazi guard. "It was an act of revenge on the Poles for having given her away," Beta wrote. "Her act gave that man courage to survive."

Even then I had some murky knowledge of a truth that was to clarify in later years: Helen valued active death over a victim's life, and in her act she celebrated the dignity of life and affirmed the will to survive. As a Jew, she had to be governed by a doctrine that is central to our faith: "Therefore choose life, that thou and thy seed shall live."

> We dance to songs
> in a world below ice, below time,
> sleepwalk to laws
> that manage our acts,

I wrote years later in a poem, "Letter to Helen," assuming that she believed in the biblical injunction whether or not she could summon it to memory. At the same time, the life she chose was built on a sequence of deeds, one following the other in a cause-and-effect relationship. She opted for the precarious life of a Jewish medical student in Warsaw; she elected to bear the hazards of Poland; and she risked her life to save her young patients. In choosing death, she held for the highest life she knew.

At the time the news of Helen restored reason to us in New

York. The facts did not lessen the impact of either the Holocaust or our personal loss, but they gave us a way to deal with both. My father's knowledge of Helen's death enabled him to read about other disasters. His silences abated as he examined the newspaper accounts, studied the Black Books, and began to absorb the extent of destruction. Although his scars were never to heal, he did resume a buoyant life. I remember him during those years of restoration. He would send roses and a book to a new friend or try to play a Chopin Nocturne and, recognizing failure, leap up and coax my mother and me to accompany him to Carnegie Hall. In time he grew well.

As for me, the distorted, dreamlike images of the Holocaust gave way to waking realities that were painful in other ways. At the war's end, when I first heard the word "Holocaust," translated then from the French *"L'holocauste,"* I thought of a monster with a *"hollow caste,"* which, in one of the languages I could not learn, meant no face and no name, who came out of a bog and avenged himself by changing people into fragments of one body, faceless, voiceless, nameless. Defending us against it were comic-strip fighters with X-ray guns who would protect our Government and its Laws, Democracy and its Institutions, and Freedom. I saw life as a struggle between social morality and supernatural evil, a battle enacted in headlines and radio broadcasts.

As the details of horror accumulated force, I saw the monster with the "hollow caste" change into an evil system. The nameless mass altered to become victims, people slaughtered by actual people. Helen's deed had transformed our fantasies because she asserted her name. She fought back. She refused to be brought low. Her act offered a clear view of what we could not imagine. It gave us words for the unutterable.

As far as I dare speculate on matters of influence, I would say that Helen's death had much to do with my being a writer, but little to do with the kind of writer I became. Her fierce individuality enabled me to see myself and every other being as distinct from any other. My early fantasy of the victim as one solid mass of flesh changed, after her noble death, to a picture of separate bodies, torn, defiled, and desecrated, but human.

Nevertheless, her culture was not my culture. Her lofty example was no more aesthetic than my father's melodic recitations in Polish and German were literary experiences, sustaining though they were. A child of my time and place, I wrote out of gratitude to works that were composed in English and to the icons and the frescoes that had inspired them. I remember visiting a synagogue when I was a child and hearing in prayers a passionate sorrow I wanted to capture in language. My way of transforming that quality of sorrow was through English accents and rhythms, learned from Donne, Herbert, and, especially, Hopkins:

Mine, O thou Lord of life, send my roots rain.

It is a commonplace that one's deepest voice is that of another. I became myself when, hearing the music of Hopkins, I wrote in the voice of a Jew named Helen, praising life in her manner.

Helen's act taught me an integrity that was threatened during the postwar years. My enemy then was a steamroller like the radical "metaphysical" image in Marianne Moore's poem, one that would "crush all the particles down / into close conformity, and then walk back and forth on them." It was a time when people were pressed into molds according to social utility: Women were thought to pursue writing only when they were free from household chores; men were poured into casts labeled "provider" and "authority."

My parents proclaimed their Jewish heritage despite the backlash from fellow workers who made stereotypes of Jews and other minorities. I remember one of my father's visits to anti-Semitic clients, cotton-mill manufacturers in Durham, North Carolina. For months he had chafed at representing the mill owner, who accepted my father because he did not detect in him characteristics he disparaged. This gracious bigot invited my father to his home and announced that customarily he honored guests by asking them to say grace before evening meals. He called on my father, who reached for a silk, hand-rolled handkerchief, knotted it at the corners, placed it on his head, and said, *"Baruch atah adonai . . ."* then continued the prayer to the end. His host was startled but curious. "It's the original," my father intoned. His handkerchief reminded me of Helen's Polish flag and all it taught us about the need to stand fast.

My father's assertion was no upheaval, but it did the job, and perhaps its modest scale was the only one suitable to his way of life. An actor turned businessman, he was at once alive to self-expression and bound by custom, torn between his sympathy for those in misery and his commitment to the necessities of his world. Although I understood his dilemma, I knew that I could never accept such a burden.

In the 1960s, when I was in graduate school, there was less pressure to conform. Patriotism, too, was less compelling. Even before Vietnam, the war in Korea, for example, had thrown to doubt the faith in a system that would set things right and the wisdom of trading lives for doctrine. The news of brutality from trusted sources lowered the status of what we called heroism. Abnormal prowess was suspect, for it was clear that World War II was the last war for which a rationale could be found. And still, even as we aired our conviction that peace was the only acceptable standard, the Vietnam War grew out of control and beyond the range of our protests. For years we felt estranged.

For my own poems, it was a time of crisis. To write of events that mattered, I had to maintain my trust in human rightness. I wanted to create grounds for hope and to invent reasons for confidence in worthy men and women. Around me artists, suffering for the oppressed, tried to rid their work of the imagery and archetypes that spoke for uniqueness. On the contrary, I had to believe in heroism. For me, song was praise.

For heroes I turned inward, to my imagination and to literature. My standard was Beowulf, the ruler of the Anglo-Saxon epic, who was, I believe, an exemplar of peace. Never appearing in battle scenes between human warriors, Beowulf fights not men but demons who visit evil on mankind. He destroys Grendel and, in an underwater cave, Grendel's mother, both fiends that are devouring the people; he slays a firedragon that has ravaged the country; he kills sea monsters that attack him while he swims to Finland. Beowulf ("bee-keeper") protects order against the monsters that threaten it, monsters that, in modern terms, can be seen as violent components of the self, irrational impulses that come up from some rank place and must be defeated. I knew him to be a defender of tranquility in a poem that cried peace even in times of slaughter.

Beowulf moves me to this day. In recent years I saw in the

British Museum glass cases filled with objects belonging to a seventh-century Anglo-Saxon king who may have been a prototype of Beowulf. The objects were found in the remains of a large boat in August 1939—curiously just before the blitzkrieg that preceded the war—at Sutton Hoo, on Suffolk's River Deben, near the North Sea.

Another of my fictional heroes was the protagonist of Bertolt Brecht's *Mother Courage,* the black marketeer in a corrupt system who sacrifices her own humanity to survive. Her daughter Kattrin, on the other hand, a mute who cannot overcome her virtuous impulses, climbs a ladder, sits on a roof, and plays a drum to warn the people of the enemy's approach. She is shot down. While Mother Courage finds ways of evading the evil system, innocent Kattrin confronts it. Her act is useless in a collective world, a world of victims.

At the time I considered the term "heroism" in the traditional sense as an aesthetic designation, rather than to describe good deeds in the modern world. In classical tragedy, the hero is not simply a morally inspiring man or woman, but is one who holds fast to some permanent value beyond our practical needs. A hero's act might alter our existence and affirm the cosmic order. The heroes of Sophocles, for example, protest against the limitations of being merely human. Each of them struggles with a "necessity," greater than any social problem, that acknowledges life's smallness and is defeated by a "destiny" that is intrinsic to his character. The hero falls knowing, and restores universal harmony.

Since then the notion of heroism has remained a luminous question. If the hero of classical tragedy is one who transforms the cosmic order, there is a notable lack of accord today as to what that order might be. People of different ideologies will disagree about stature. Recently, though, I have been attracted to deeds that affirm integrity in a world that would urge conformity. The hero's search for identity would be futile today in a society that encourages uniformity. Although no person can affect collective history, perhaps the outstanding individual can withstand those pressures and retain a singular vision.

When I consider that quest for identity, I think of Helen. What distinguishes her for me is that I remember her name, and I will. Her act was iconic, for it drew the imagination and engaged the memory. Her achievement was to be permanent, for it depended on her absolute conviction of right and wrong.

I picture her, always, standing on that roof, holding the torn Polish flag, knowing she would be shot or would leap to her death. Her gesture saved no one, nor did it alter the social order, let alone the cosmic one. Nor was her stance a protest in the name of an ideology. If she inspired other sufferers, I doubt that it was her goal. Helen was simply being what she was and doing what she had to do. She could not accept a passive death. She declined to walk, naked, to her death. The indignity of a concentration camp was a price she could not pay, not even for the hope of staying alive. Her very freedom, in fact, had forced her to climb those steps to her death, as though inertness had become repellent to her sense of life as a series of committed choices, and sinful to the conscience that sense had created.

Instructed by her example, my father did what he had to do, modestly but well. As for me, I learned from Helen's uniqueness the value of selfhood. Her courage established the importance of the freedom to act. As a link in a chain of faces, voiceless and nameless, I could not speak. Only with my face, my voice, and my name could I even begin to grope in the dark for words.

The Story of the Creation Poet

"In the beginning, God created the heaven and the earth." So opens the story in which God calls into being light, land and sea, fish, animals, men and women. In verses of pure wonder, the tone is achieved paradoxically by the negation of wonder. The God that is known through his words has a voice that is never heard directly—and that is its power. The narrator of this mightiest of all deeds is a recorder whose modesty ironically heightens the drama. The account is set forth simply and clearly, with an unexpected bareness of utterance. The poet has muted personal emotion to emphasize the miracle of God's handiwork, the force of God's supreme commands, and the speed with which they are fulfilled: "And God said, Let there be light: and there was light."

The poet's artistry is staggering. The evaluation that follows God's creation of light, "And God saw the light, that it was good," certainly is meiotic, or ironically understated. Although "good" has a greater range of meaning in the Hebrew of Genesis than in English, it is still in the subdued narrator's tone. But the understatement changes to marvel when it is used as a refrain, "And God saw that it was good . . ." occurring five times at the ends of verses and varied in the first chapter's final verse: "And God saw every thing he made, and behold, it was very good." Further, "it was good" alternates with "it was so," both accenting the jobs done swiftly and well. Those repetitions build throughout the passage. They grow louder, characterizing the narrator as not simply detached but controlled. Finally, he is filled with pent-up emotion. God is pleased; the narrator is

This essay appeared in *Genesis: As It Is Written,* edited by David Rosenberg (San Francisco: HarperCollins, 1996).

astonished. The image of Creation is made to shine forth with feelings that remain unspoken.

The process of Creation is mysterious. Elsewhere in Genesis, God's technical instructions are precise: Noah's ark, for example, is made of gopher wood, is three hundred cubits in length, three stories high, with a skylight and a side entrance (6:14–16). Here, though, God speaks, names, and, without further effort or blueprint, "it was so." In the only passage when God announces what is to come, "Let us make man in our own image," the intention is expanded, even glorified, with the addition of "after our likeness," emphasizing the holiness of "image" and implying the intended legacy of godly purity. Directly after those words, God gives man and woman custody of the earth and of all things in it.

That dexterity is found throughout the brief passage. Overall, there is a pleasing formal symmetry: Creation's six-day process is divided into two groups, the first of the elements, and the second of those using them. In each three-day group, the first day has a single deed (light, heavenly lights); the second has a deed split into two parts (heaven and earth; birds and fish); the third has two distinct creations (dry land and sea, animals and human beings). By the first three verses of chapter 2 ("and God blessed the seventh day") God is delighted and exhausted. This is the last, and best, of the many worlds God has created and thrown away—310, according to legend. God, the foremost artist, is an inveterate reviser. So must be the Creation poet.

To dramatize God's rule, the poet juxtaposes such great opposites as heaven and earth, morning and evening, day and night. The writer's musical effects—refrains, parallelisms, and repetitive parallelisms—start here and resonate throughout the Hebrew Bible. Recurrences of "it was good" and "it was so" are interspersed with another refrain, "And the evening and the morning were the first day," the number varying with each repetition.

The theme of fecundity is strengthened by parallels, or phrases in which like images glorify abundance: "And the earth brought forth grass, and herb yielding seed after its kind, and the tree yielding fruit, whose seed was in itself." It is further emphasized by repetitive parallels, or those same phrases made to recur, resulting in lines crowded with strong, persistent images. These bolster God's creation of the foliage and, later, of the animals:

> And God said, Let the earth bring forth the living creature after his kind, cattle, and creeping thing, and beast of the earth after his kind. . . . And God made the beast of the earth after his kind, and cattle after their kind, and every thing that creepeth upon the earth after his kind: and God saw that it was good.

By far God's highest blessing is fertility. Throughout the Hebrew Bible the theme returns: life after our kind is our immortality. Over and again, vital figures gain, are cheated of, and regain the right to extend their lives through progeny and more progeny. In the Creation story, God instructs creatures to continue life's ongoing beauty. It is merely an expectation for the fruit tree "yielding fruit, whose seed was in itself, after his kind." For fish, birds, and human beings, it is a divine award: "Be fruitful, and multiply, and fill the waters of the seas," and the gift is intensified by the device of parallelism.

"Be fruitful and multiply," the initial words of God's command to the fish and the birds, is repeated in the order to men and women. In contrast, though, God's blessing on men and women follows directly the creation of man "in our own image." Moreover, when God exhorts human beings to be fertile and increase, the charge accompanies additional obligations— namely, the subordination of all other living things. Although the command seems shocking in our time, it assumes the model conduct of an untarnished prelapsarian world. I read the passage now for an ironic awareness that only the Supreme Being achieves godly perfection:

> And God blessed them, and God said unto them, be fruitful, and multiply, and replenish the earth, and subdue it: and have dominion over the fish of the sea, and over the fowl of the air, and over every living thing that moveth upon the earth.

My own enchantment with the Creation story began when I read of Caedmon, the elderly untaught farmhand who became our first poet. Caedmon's "Hymn," the first poem in English, is about the Creation. Caedmon's story is told by Bede, an eighth-century English historian who wrote mostly in Latin. Bede narrated miracles as well as historical facts, both in precise detail.

Caedmon worked in the fields near Whitby Abbey, a setting that matches the strangeness of this story. The abbey, when I visited it, was lodged high on a moor in Yorkshire, not far from the sea. To walk those heather-filled craters is to lose one's way, look up at dizzying horizons, and see, in that lunar country, the windowless skull that was Whitby. And even if Whitby has changed since seventh-century England, certain remarkable things remain: for one thing, there were those wild moors in which Caedmon perceived order; for another, Whitby was one of the double monasteries of men and women that marked the Anglo-Saxon Church. Hild, a woman, was abbess.

By nature, Caedmon resembles the restrained narrator of the Creation story. Unable to learn verses, too shy to sing at a feast where guests were required to improvise, Caedmon fled to a barn to care for the horses. He fell asleep and dreamed "a person" commanded him to sing the origin of things. On waking, he remembered the dream words:

> Nu sculon herigean   heofonrices weard
> metodes meahte   and his modgethanc
> weorc wuldoraedor   swa he wundra gehes
>
> Now we shall praise   heaven's keeper
> the maker's might   and his mind's thought
> father of the world   as of all wonder

That is the opening of Caedmon's "Hymn." When the Abbess Hild heard of it, she invited Caedmon to instruct the monks in prayer. Thereafter, he continued to write verses that suited the monastery, modeling his language on the war songs of the royal meadhalls. Bede's account—that "someone," presumably an angel, commanded Caedmon to sing—always struck me as the human tendency to find a concrete reason for the artist's power that eludes reason.

Caedmon's method bears watching. He writes of God's Creation in Anglo-Saxon, the language of a pagan culture. The creation story Caedmon had known was in the Bible translation of his time, Saint Jerome's fourth-century Vulgate text. The poems he had heard were the monks' Latin prayer chants at Whitby, and, in contrast, the battle songs sung by scops, or local bards, about the warlords they served.

In his Creation hymn, Caedmon used the scops' epithets for king: "keeper," "ruler," "lord." At the same time, he used adjectives ("heaven," "lord") to qualify the epithets. Had he, in reverse, sung of war in Latin, he would not have been the first English poet. Indeed, the result might have ranged from mediocrity to disaster. Instead, he composed his great song by fusing the rock-hard, brawny *language* of war with the noble *matter* of God's Creation. Throughout literature we find masterful ways of combining sacred and secular, doctrine and language, such as, for example, Dante's use of the vernacular for his sacred subject. It strikes me here that Caedmon was alert to the sameness, rather than the differences, of the two cultures, by combining pictures and words. To depict Creation, he uses "maker" and "father" as marvelous puns. He plays with language: if king is lord, then God is King; if king is keeper, then God is heaven's keeper.

The Anglo-Saxon poet's story reminds me of my grandfather's musical practice. A Hungarian Jew, he was a lawyer who sang for his father, a cantor in a synagogue in New York's Lower East Side. My grandfather sang the liturgy to tunes he had heard in music halls. His favorite tune, "There's *one* New York, there is but *one* New York," was sung in a bar by a woman named Bessie, who wore tights; to this melody he fit the Sabbath prayer's words, "Le *ha* dodi le *krat* shalat," based on the Song of Solomon. What he did was at least another step in the ongoing aesthetic process of transforming the liturgy and popular culture.

Caedmon's hymn is central to my life. I memorized it when, during a hiatus between college and graduate school, I worked as a newspaper reporter covering a police beat on *The Alexandria Gazette,* a northern Virginia daily. My notes on current events were immediate, urgent—and transient. So much for the present. I longed to read literature of the past, which would leave an indelible mark on the future.

In that dislocation, after a long silence, I wrote of Caedmon and his hymn. In my poem, Hild overheard him sing and, knowing he was uneducated, attributed his inspiration to an angel's visit. I imagined Caedmon leaving a banquet where the gleemen sang battle songs of the kings they served. Too shy to perform there, he fled to a barn and sang the Creation.

More recently, I've been drawn to *Bereshit*, the Hebrew name for Genesis. Literally meaning "At the beginning of," it comprises the first words of the text. The word is magical, for it implies all origins. Undoubtedly prebiblical Talmudic legends of God's Creation through the letter B are ancestors of Genesis.

The Creation poet is the unacknowledged master of integrating the sacred and the secular, using the legends and languages of at least two cultures. The Hebrew Genesis bears a startling resemblance to an earlier Babylonian epic, "enuma elish," or "When on High." In fact, the two texts share precise details. E. A. Speiser, whose translation of Genesis appears in the Anchor Bible, points out that the order of events is the same in both texts, a fact that argues for the Hebrew having borrowed from the Mesopotamian source. In both accounts, the sequence is divine spirit; chaos and darkness; the creations of light, firmament, dry land, luminaries, man. The crucial difference is that in the Babylonian epic, everything emanates from the gods, and on the seventh day the gods rest and celebrate. In the Hebrew Bible, there is one God. Where Caedmon uses biblical myth for his Anglo-Saxon hymn, the Creation poet writes in Hebrew, using the details of the Babylonian cosmic legend and a monotheistic God. Both Caedmon and the Creation poet are attentive less to the differences between cultures and doctrines than to the images they share—Caedmon's God as King arises from biblical myth plus the Anglo-Saxon kings and gods; the Creation poet's array of images and the idea of divinity are used to sing one God.

The Creation story tells of goodness everywhere. The stability of the single God—as opposed to the capriciousness of the many gods—has to do with that perfection. Later in Genesis, there will be evil. After the fall from Eden, which was based on deliberate choice, God's selection process narrows gradually, from Noah who is saved and Shem who is blessed to Abraham who is elect and Isaac who is chosen. Here at the start, though, there is universal justice and order.

For me, the single God that distinguishes the Hebrew Bible

from the version or versions that preceded it signifies the single consciousness required by a work of art. The Creation is an image of the exemplary artist who lives, in Frost's words, "by turning to fresh tasks," making what will never be undone. He examines the raw material and shapes it—"the dry land," "the evening and the morning," "the tree yielding fruit"—then transforms it by commanding the work into being. It is done. He is pleased and somewhat startled by what is there. And the figure is presented by a poet who, after a long silence, awakens and sees things once deemed ordinary as miracles.

Song of Songs

Love Is Strong as Death

In a magnificent passage, "My Beloved Spake" (2:10–16), a woman, who is the dominant character in the Song of Solomon (so-called in the King James or Authorized Version), recounts her lover's rousing words: "Rise up, my love, my fair one, and come away." The six verses, taken as a unit, are characteristic of the Song as a whole, which is concerned with a man and a woman who, with heightened sensations of sight and smell, taste and touch, celebrate each other's beauty just as they praise the hills and animals, the trees and flowers of Israel in spring.

The section prefigures the Old French *reverdie*, a poem that glorifies new love and the green earth. Here the device of parallelism strengthens the amorous plea, as in the lines in which a series of phrases with like images amplify spring's return, the last illustration locating the subdued birdsong in the country of the man and the woman, emphasizing the growing relationship between them and the landscape.

The passage ends with a refrain, or "distant" repetition, "My beloved is mine, and I am his: he feedeth among the lilies," a verse that introduces a shift in tone and imagery, in the time of day, and in emotion. Throughout the Song, lines that recur with variations set off such changes.

"My beloved spake" and the Song as a whole tell of awakening to a rising green world in its fullness, with renewed hope. The tactile yet transient figures of birds, vines, figs, and lilies, and the repeated verb forms in the present tense, call forth a

Originally published in *Congregation: Contemporary Writers Read the Jewish Bible,* edited by David Rosenberg (New York: Harcourt, Brace, 1987).

creation story, a genesis, a tale of new beginnings. Often the imagery is unmistakably sexual, with emphasis on smell and taste ("Let my beloved come into the garden, and eat his pleasant fruits" [4:16]; "thy breasts shall be as clusters of the vine" [7:8]; "let us see if the vine flourish, whether the tender grape appear" [7:12]). The physical imagery, though, however graphic, is rendered generative by a vulnerable, even animal-like, manner of discovery. The earth is burgeoning; people and animals are coming into themselves and into one another's love.

At the same time, the book is built on an alternating pattern of ecstasy in daylight scenes and loss at night. "My beloved spake" immediately precedes one of the dark passages, in which the joyful address, early in the poem, "O thou whom my soul loveth" (1:7), is repeated and varied as "I sought him whom my soul loveth: I sought him, but found him not" (3:1). Strengthening the repetitive wish for love that is genuine, but that may be transitory, are the strategic refrains or distant repetitions ("Rise up, my love, my fair one," "Arise my love, my fair one" [2:10, 13]); the epanaleptic repetitions, in which words are taken up again after intervening words ("let me see thy countenance, let me hear thy voice; for sweet is thy voice, and thy countenance is comely"); and the acervate clusters of detail that focus attention on the characters' longing.

Passion and danger are the terrifying polarities of the Song. Passages such as "My beloved spake" are balanced by verses that intimate devastation, as in one that recurs with variations:

> Who is she that looketh forth as the morning, fair as the
> moon, clear as the sun, and terrible as an army with
> banners? (6:10)

and death:

> Set me as a seal upon thine heart, as a seal upon thine arm:
> for love is strong as death; jealousy is cruel as the grave:
> the coals thereof are coals of fire, which hath a most vehe-
> ment flame. (8:6, 7)

In the first of those verses, the final phrase comes as a surprise, the woman's power changing to destruction in the eyes of the man, who utters the lines. In the second verse, also spoken by the man, the parallel phrases are doubled: assertions and amplifications are qualified, each term having two parts, resulting in lines that are crowded with strong images.

Passion is fierce; love is strong as death and will triumph despite fears, ambivalence, and life's decay. Love, tenacious as death, conquers the inevitable; passion, harsh as death, simultaneously terrifies and endures. Seemingly opposed, love and death have, in fact, one name. Although the Song's characters salute life and love, the work does not iterate life's mutability. Those grim lines, at the climax of the poem, convey the startling truth that love is only apparently transient, but actually eternal.

One of the shortest books in the Bible, second only to the Book of Ruth in its brevity, the Song has inspired libraries of comment. For centuries scholars have debated the date of composition, which ranges from Solomonic times to the fifth century B.C.E.,[1] the allegorical interpretations, the question of plot, and other considerations. The Hebrew title, שיר השירים אשר לשלמה, translated as "Song of Songs, which is Solomon's," is a superlative, as in "king of kings" or "vanity of vanities." The book is also called Canticles, which comes from the Latin Vulgate rendering of Canticum Canticorum.

Erotic as it is, the Song is the first of the Five *Megillot,* or Scrolls, preceding Ruth, Lamentations, Ecclesiastes, and Esther, and is read on the eighth day of Passover. Although the book has no explicit mention of God, and has neither overt theological doctrine nor apparent national theme, it was taken into the canon largely because of its allegorical interpretation, that of the lover-bridegroom as God, and the Shulamite-bride as Israel. This level of meaning, which is accepted even today by many serious readers, was defended near the close of the first century C.E. by Rabbi Akiba, who cursed anyone taking the words literally, but who, on the other hand, called the Song of Songs the "Holy of Holies."[2] Just why he did so is uncertain: he may have been referring to the Song's mystical connotations, or to his conviction that marital love was sacred because it awakened a more profound love of God. His phrase seems ironic now, for it echoes the superscripture, and presents as religious the love songs that scholars, centuries later, have deemed profane. Still, the Synagogue received the Song of Songs early, if not without debate. The Christian Church accepted the allegorical interpretation as well, understanding the symbolic meaning to be Christ and his Church.

Marvin H. Pope's intriguing conviction is that the origins of the Song are in the sacred sexual rites of ancient Near Eastern fertility cults, which celebrated, often with eating, drinking, and copulation, the life in death and the continuity of life.[3] He refers often to the Tammuz cult, or, in Babylonian religion, the worship of a young god loved by the moon goddess, Ishtar, who kills him but restores him to life. His festival, commemorating the annual death and rebirth of vegetation, corresponds to that of Adonis. This cultic view, likening the woman to Ishtar, Aphrodite, and Anat, does clarify her role in the Song as the initiator, whose viewpoint, even when distorted by pain or by passion, compels us to see things as she does.

In literary terms, the Song is not, strictly speaking, allegory, since the other *(allos)* meaning is not implicit in the text, and because there are multiple levels of meaning. Allegory, as distinguished from ambiguity, is a structural principle and depends upon a continuous use of imagery that refers to a set of ideas.

The question is important here because it governs language. The woman declares, for example, that her love "shall be all night betwixt my breasts" (1:13). There, allegorical and eclectic readings might be at variance with it, as we learn in Midrash Rabbah, the image refers to Abraham's head clasped between the Divine Presence and the angel, or, as in the work of an early Christian expositor, the image presents a man's head enclosed by the Hebrew Bible and the Gospels. On the other hand, words such as "garden," "vines," "tender grape," "myrrh," "rising," "navel" bear religious and sexual connotations, in addition to their denotative meanings as natural objects. The difference between the two kinds of images is, in fact, one small fissure in the vast chasm between allegory and ambiguity.

Nor do I mean to dismiss an allegorical purpose in a work that has carried varied readings so gracefully. New interpretations have increased the fascination for a book whose prevailing tone is wonder: the lovers marvel at the intensity of their passion and at the splendor of the natural world. As though in sympathy with their mystification, scholars and critics have questioned incessantly the origin of the book, the identity of the characters, and the unity.

The theories range from the Song as a protest against the urban life of the early Israelites to a text for modern psychological dream-interpretation. Although some readings seem irrelevant to the Song's aesthetic import, a few are worth noting. To begin with irrelevance, a theory involving a coherent plot, with a shepherd and a royal bridegroom competing for the bride, has been discarded, by and large, because there is no allusion to rivalry in the text, and because there is no structural progression that would support that reading. Although Solomon is named in the title, it is unlikely that he wrote the book, and he is not an active character in it. Instead, the references to him are probably invocations of a royal ideal of beauty.

The "wedding-week theory," proposed in the last century by J. G. Wetstein with respect to Syrian villagers and by von Kremer regarding Lebanese people, holds that the Song rests on ancient Syrian-Palestinian marriage customs. Although the proposals have been disputed, because those traditions were not found to exist earlier than the nineteenth century and because parts of the Song, notably the reverie chants (three and five), are hardly wedding pieces, the notion does bear on the Song's style. One custom is that the bride, on her wedding eve, performs a sword dance, which would be a likely accompaniment for chant seven ("How beautiful are thy feet"). The book's royal imagery suggests the nineteenth-century—but not earlier, apparently—practice in which the couple, during the wedding week, are celebrated as "king" and "queen," with village maidens attending the bride, and townspeople forming a regal procession singing praises to the physical radiance of the bridal pair.

The concept of recent decades is that these are secular verses, concerned only with human love. Although that perception ensures a compelling reading, it does not account for the godlike stature of the man ("his countenance is as Lebanon, excellent as the cedars" [5:15]), or the goddess quality of the woman ("I am the rose of Sharon" [2:1]), or the woman's unquestioning generosity with regard to others who worship her man ("there-fore do the virgins love thee" [1:3]); nor does it explain the re-ligious meaning it has had for early and modern readers.

In reading the Song as literature, I regard the allegorical and cultic elements as allusions that expand or enlarge the central human characters, radiating out from them. When the woman, in chant one, speaks of her lover as "the king," she praises a man with allusive shadows of Solomon, YHWH, Christ, the Syrian bridegroom, Tammuz, Adonis, Baal. When the man sings, "Thou art all fair, my love" (4:7), he worships a lady with qualities, real or imagined, that are allusions to those of Ishtar, the Shekinah, Mary, Aphrodite, Anat, Astarte, and, of course, the people of Israel. The reading I find most relevant to the poem's great achievement is that the mythological and religious figures heighten, rather than become, the central characters.

The man, primarily, sings in fantastic images that objectify his happiness and veiled fear ("Thy neck is as a tower of ivory" [7:4]; "Thy neck like the tower of David" [4:4]). The luminous, hyperbolic images are reminiscent of conceits bearing antithet-ical elements, which are common in love poetry and in devo-tional verse, as in, for example, "A Description" by Lord Herbert of Cherbury, in which the lover compares his lady's neck to an atlas; or in "The Odour" by George Herbert, in which the speaker perceives the divine voice as a fragrance.

In the Song, though, the outlandish images are equivalents for inner perceptions of what is the purest, the strangest, the most glorious. I am reminded of the Gedullat Mosheh, a small midrash devoted entirely to Moses' journey to heaven. In it he sees streams of water, celestial windows marked "war" and "peace," angels with seventy thousand heads, and seraphim with calves' feet. In the highest heaven, Moses finds two angels, each five hundred parasangs tall (one parasang equals three miles) and forged out of chains of black fire and red fire.[4] The outsize images have affinities, also, to those in the *Hekhaloth* books that cover a period of one thousand years, from the first century B.C.E. to the tenth C.E.[5] Vividly recorded there are journeys of *Merkabah* mystics, a group that included the Song's early de-fender, Rabbi Akiba (Akiba ben Joseph).

The mystic attained, through fasting and prayer, a condition of self-oblivion. Then, actually seated, head between knees, but inwardly ascending to the palaces in the highest of seven heavens, he had to fend off hostile demons opposed to the soul's liberation. The journey was splendid in its promise of perfection, frightening in its dangers, and terrifying in the underlying knowledge that the traveler must fall to earth. Such are the heights and falls of the Song.

Another kind of imagery in the poem is based on the form of the Arabic *wasf*, a descriptive song in praise of the beloved. Usually the poem has an affirmative introduction, as in the *wasf* of chant four ("Behold, thou art fair, my love"); comparisons, as in the anaphoral lines that follow ("Thy teeth are like . . . Thy lips are like . . . Thy neck is like . . ."); and clusters of detail that control passion by objectifying it. The maiden's sword dance in chant seven is performed to a *wasf* that is sung by the man.

Although the *wasf* is very old, it has survived to our day. I think of a *wasf* in a recent anthology called *Modern Poetry of the Arab World*, translated by Abdullah al-Udhari. The poem "Rain Song" by Badr Shakir Al Sayyab (1926–64) opens:

> Your eyes are palm groves refreshed by dawn's breath
> Or terraces the moon leaves behind.
> When your eyes smile the vines flower
> And the lights dance
> Like the moon's reflection on a river
> Gently sculled at the crack of dawn
> Like stars pulsating in the depth of your eyes
> That sink in mists of grief like the sea
> Touched by the evening's hands. . . .[6]

Modern Israeli love songs, on the other hand, often incorporate present-day displacements of tradition, making ironic use of the Song. In Yehuda Amichai's poem "Love's Gifts," the lover declares:

> I comforted you with apples, as it says
> in the Song of Songs,
> I lined your bed with them,
> so we could roll smoothly on red apple-bearings.[7]

The Song's unity is a major achievement in itself. It is the structure that reveals larger concerns, such as the gift of consciousness, the power of love, and the complexities of joy. In fact, for those who believe it is a collection of popular ditties, it is necessary to add that the unknown scribes who arranged the songs were actually editors with a redactorial genius that is rare, and even unwanted, in times of evident authorship. By studying it, verse by verse, line by line, the reader can find its symmetry, unity, and scope.

The Song is a great love poem, an extended lyric whose structure is determined by musical amplifications and variations. Its chapters, sequences of verses, are actually "chants" or rhythmic divisions. The poem modulates from theme to theme, one image suggesting another, which in turn leads to a new statement.

The structure is also psychological and is built on the emotional progress of the two characters. The joyful scenes, like the call to spring in chant two, are set in daylight, with vivid colors (green figs [2:13], the chariot's purple cover [3:10], the scarlet thread [4:3], ivory belly [5:14], pomegranates (throughout)). The sorrowful sections are set in twilight states and are in the diction and imagery of reverie, as in chants three ("By night on my bed") and five ("I sleep, but my heart waketh"). They are characterized by distorted dreamlike imagery, and by sudden, surprising leaps in tone that are associational rather than logical. Between those opposite states are happy daydreams, again marked by brightly colored images, such as the scenes that open chants two and eight, and contain the recurrent lines "His left hand is under my head," "His left hand should be under my head" (2:6, 8:3).

The poem is profoundly concerned with consciousness, and the psychological progression includes a movement from awareness to daydream, to reverie, to awareness to deeper reverie, to awareness to daydream, and back to full consciousness. Waking is central to the action: the lovers call each other to "Arise!" and to "Awake!" In a blissful scene, when the senses are acute, the woman alludes to wine "causing the lips of those that are asleep to speak" (7:9). And in the recurrent lines "I charge you, O ye daughters . . . that ye stir not up," she warns Jerusalem girls not to rouse love until it comes of its own accord. (Although some translators interpret the phrase as "my love," it is more likely that the word *ahabah,* used without the article in 2:0, 3:10, 5:8, 7:7, 8:6, and with the article, *ha'ahabah,* in 3:5, 8:4,17, means "love" itself.)

The poem is unified further in that changes in awareness are the very shifts set off by refrains, or distant repetitions, spaced widely over the eight chants. Usually those recurrent lines vary in one or more words, altering the meaning slightly, and assisting the emotional or narrative progress. They have effects similar to incremental repetition in stanzaic verse, a device found as early as in ancient Chinese poetry. One of the Song's distant repetitions is "My beloved is mine, and I am his," "I am my beloved's, and my beloved is mine," "I am my beloved's, and his desire is toward me" (2:16, 6:3, 7:10), all spoken by the woman. The first, ending the passage "My beloved spake," indicates a change from daylight and rapture to night and loss; the second sets off the transition from a man who is absent to a man who returns but is apprehensive ("Thou art beautiful . . . comely . . . terrible as an army with banners"), and the third precedes his peaceful resolution ("Come, my beloved, let us go forth into the field"). Another of the distant repetitions is "My beloved is like a roe or a young hart," "Be thou like to a roe or a young hart upon the mountains of Bether," "Be thou like to a roe or a young hart upon the mountains of spices" (2:9, 17; 8:14). First the image appears as an inquisitive animal; next it calls forth a rapid shift to night in lines that introduce the first reverie, with its pain of loss; in the third instance it closes the book.

Also patterning the long poem is the device of repetitive parallelism, or the use of lines that recur without intervening text. Some verses are both repetitive parallels and distant repetitions, such as "Behold thou art fair" (1:15, 16; 4:1, 7). The first of these verses leads into the woman's daydream in chant two; the second introduces the man's disquieted courtship; the third ushers in his call to flee to the mountains.

Another unifying principle is the depiction of one leading character throughout. It seems remarkable, too, that an active woman is the chief suitor of this ancient love song. Her yearning is the most poignant. She calls, beckons, cajoles, pursues. The Song opens and closes with expressions of her desire: "Let him kiss me with the kisses of his mouth," and "Make haste, my beloved." (Incidentally, the enallage, or shift in persons, in 1:2 makes her love appear godlike, at least to the woman; actually, though, the usage occurs frequently in biblical verse.) Boldly she expresses her longing: "Comfort me with apples: for I am sick of love" (2:5; or, I faint for love), she exclaims. Proudly she declares: "I am a wall and my breasts are towers" (8:10); "I am black, but comely" (1:5); "I am the rose of Sharon, and the lily of the valleys" (2:1), a verse whose erotic implications are amplified by the recurrent image of lilies among which her lover feeds. She courts the man: "Let my beloved come into his garden, and eat his pleasant fruits." In the night reverie chants she leaves her bed to find him (chant three), then leaves her bed to find him gone (chant five).

Complementing her development in the poem is the progress of the man, who, in contrast, is acted upon. Although both declare their longing, she is the braver, he the more timidly withdrawn. He is baffled by his own response to her beauty, complaining, "Thou hast ravished my heart with one of thine eyes" (4:9). He pictures her and their love in images of combat. In chant four, depicting his lady as the ideal beauty, flawless, with perfect teeth and lips, he presents her also in images of defensive weapons at rest: shields, "the tower of David builded for an armoury" (4:4). In his vision, distorted by terror, his beloved is cool, aloof, "a spring shut up." When he disappears, the young women of Jerusalem, who may be bridesmaids according to the "wedding-week" theory, or simply companions, join their friend in her quest, asking, "whither is thy beloved turned aside? that we may seek him with thee" (6:1).

Because of her beauty and mastery, the woman evokes curiosity. More details are provided, but they are all the more intriguing for their ambiguity. The woman's assertion "I am black" has prototypes ranging from the black madonnas in churches of Europe to the Indian goddess Kali, whose name means "black" and who is carnal but violent. Robert Graves observes that many statues of virgins in Spain and southern France are black because the Saracen occupation during the Middle Ages taught local Christians to consider blackness wise.[8] I believe these are best regarded as allusions that radiate from the central figures, elevating them and intensifying their plight. In terms of the Song's pattern of imagery, though, the statement distinguishes her as being uncommon, rare, out of the ordinary. On the other hand, her lover is fair and ruddy, with raven-black hair.

Her song, "Look not upon me, because I am black" (1:6), rises and soars, sent aloft by a double parallel structure, the second and third phrases amplifying the first assertion, and the fifth and sixth phrases clarifying the third, "my mother's children." Displeased with her, those children made her "keeper of the vineyards; but mine own vineyard have I not kept." Throughout the Song, vines, gardens, foliage are sexual, sometimes flagrantly so, and procreative, when preceded by "my" and "her." The woman has been deprived of love ("sick of love"), and, thus far, of the opportunity to continue the life cycle.

The portrait of the woman, which awakens attention from the beginning, acquires depth in chant three, the first of the passages in the mode of psychic experience that involve for the woman and for the reader the whole of the sensibility. Her inner struggle here and in chant five, both set at night, are characterized by the "rhetoric" of consciousness, which is conveyed by sudden leaps in thought, by irony, and by expanded, dreamlike images. Her arousal ("I will rise now" [3:2]) is presented in ironic contrast to the awakening in "My beloved spake" ("Rise up, my love, my fair one, and come away"). In the later episode, the woman, alone in bed, yearns for her love. Her desire is compelling, although it is probably based on fancy, rather than experience, for the law forbade premarital fulfillment.

The woman's lament in chant three, in the diction of reverie, is reinforced by a beautiful repetitive parallel that has a distant repetition as well: "By night on my bed I sought him whom my soul loveth: I sought him, but I found him not," and "in the broad ways I will seek him whom my soul loveth: I sought him, but I found him not," and, recurring in the second night chant, "I sought him, but I could not find him" (3:1, 2; 5:6). The two night pieces enclose the *wasf* of chant four, sung by the man to his distant beauty, and the woman's seductive proposal. The scene moves rapidly from day to night in chant five, as well, and the woman deplores her loss: "I sleep, but my heart waketh" (5:2).

The imagery in both night scenes is extended beyond waking logic, but is precisely in keeping with reverie's exaggerated dimensions: "Who is this that cometh out of the wilderness like pillars of smoke, perfumed with myrrh and frankincense, with all powders of the merchant?" she asks in three (3:6). Describing Solomon's wedding bed, she pictures servants with swords that protect against "fear in the night" or the bad dreams she knows well. To be sure, there are historical theories for this imagery, such as the explanation that the smoke is incense from a wedding cortege that is guarded against bandits. Such reasons, though, fail to account for the vitality of the two scenes built on images that move by association and that present, in their dislocation, the panic of loss.

A deeper level of consciousness distinguishes the diction and imagery of chant five, the second night section. Here the woman, alone, undressed, hears her love knocking at the door, his hair filled with dew. She rises to meet him, her hands wet with myrrh. He is gone. He does not answer her quietly desperate call. She describes her absent love in magnified proportions: "His legs are as pillars of marble, set upon sockets of fine gold: his countenance is as Lebanon, excellent as the cedars." The hyperbole recalls the queen's dream of her lost lover, in Shakespeare's *Antony and Cleopatra*, V, ii:

> His legs bestrid the ocean; his rear'd arm
> Crested the world; his voice was propertied
> As all the tuned spheres. . . .

As in chant three, the action here is symbolic of waking behavior. The woman, who behaves frequently with the audacity of a goddess, is given to moments of reserve, and these occur dramatically in the night scenes. In chant three, she asks the city watchmen for help, then finds her beloved and grasps him firmly, but not without self-reproach. Her recurrent admonishment to the maidens, imploring them to let love follow its own course, is based on her own anguished restraint. In the second night chant, where the imagery is hallucinatory, her wish for discipline is intensified. Unexpectedly for the diction of waking narrative, but appropriately to the rhetoric of consciousness, the watchmen strip her and beat her; "the keepers of the walls took away my vail from me." She is, in her own estimation, a temple prostitute. The lady's directness, her sexual frankness, call for control: the watchmen are agents of her wish for protection against her own ardor.

The uncommon musical symmetry of this long poem is illustrated by chants six and eight, both composites of images and refrains that acquire momentum from their repetitions throughout the Song, either in repetitive parallels or in distant recurrences. In chant six, set in daylight and sung by the man, the woman, and the Jerusalem girls, we hear again, variously altered, "My beloved is gone down into his garden," "I went down into the garden," "I am my beloved's, and my beloved is mine," "Thy teeth are as a flock of sheep," "Thy hair is as a flock of goats." Again the tremulous man speaks of his love in battle images, varying the "tower of David" imagery of chant three. In lines whose destruction is emphasized by distant repetition, with variation, he asks: "Who is she that looketh forth as the morning, fair as the moon, clear as the sun, and terrible as an army with banners?"

Another sharp turn occurs with the *wasf* in chant seven, sung by the man. Often reserved, he speaks openly of his craving, without fear. He acclaims his lady's navel, comparing it to an empty goblet; her belly, likening it to wheat; and her breasts, associating them with twin roes.

Chant eight, containing the climax of the poem, begins with another of the abrupt changes in tone, this time from ecstasy to withdrawal. The woman, now cautious, wishes her love were a brother, that she might kiss him without being scorned. Just as she shrinks from boldness, the man's fright returns. Here he utters those ringing lines at the Song's climax ("Set me as a seal upon thy heart") and sings out the somber but assuring truth known to the ancients, to the gods, to the religious, and to sculptors of erotic figures on stone sarcophagi: "For love is strong as death; jealousy harsh as the grave." Love, mighty as death, is, therefore, immortal. Following that statement, the image of the little sister embodies the continuity of life and love. Like six, the chant is plangent with refrains that bind the poem together; it ends with the distant repetition that closes chant two.

Although I read the Song as a long poem concerned with human lovers and with allusions to divine and mythological figures, the literal level of this work is iridescent with ambiguity. There is the obvious analogy (not allegory) between the passion of the Song and that of any religious experience of going beyond the self to find God. The resemblance between sexual desire and divine worship is a venerable concept. For example, in Judaism as early as the twelfth century C.E. Maimonides asserted that love of God should be accompanied by constant nervous tremors, such as a man feels when he is lovesick for a woman.[9]

On the other hand, it seems a pity to miss the Song's wider implications by regarding it as being either religious or secular, without entertaining simultaneously sacred and erotic interpretations. I think of a Passover seder guest who was disconcerted by the Haggadah, illustrated by Saul Raskin, with a scroll whose Hebrew letters spelled out the first verses of the Song: "Let him kiss me with the kisses of his mouth . . ." The page was decorated with tropical flowers, a long-necked doe, and a princess whose eyes were shaped like the animal's fluent head.

I recall, too, a listener who was baffled by Henry Purcell's "My Beloved Spake," a setting of that passage. Sung by an alto, a tenor, and two basses, the polyphonic anthem had varying high and low phrases that reinforced the poem's blend of happiness and pain. The listener objected to the end of the piece, a strong round of "Hallelujahs" which is not in the text and which struck him as an abrupt tonal shift in music and language.

Actually, the Haggadah and the anthem are appropriate, according to traditional views: they are, in the first instance, the Song's prominent inclusion in the *Megillot,* and, in the second, its concern with divinely inspired human love. Apart from that, many deeply religious works are to be read with the whole of our sensibility, including physical love, and great love poems call for a spiritual reading as well. For that matter, whether we adore with our hearts or souls is a matter for endless speculation. We do not know how we cherish, but only *that* we cherish. And the Song, with its great affirmation of love's immortality, is a love poem that calls upon our deepest responses, on every level. The more its authors sing of love, the more they whisper of God.

1. The third century B.C.E. is favored by H. L. Ginsberg, "Introduction to The Song of Songs," in *The Five Megillot* (Philadelphia: The Jewish Publication Society, 1969), p. 3. Scholars are still divided, however, on the date of composition. As recently as 1973, Professor Chaim Rabin presented evidence assigning the date to Solomonic times, in "The Song of Songs and Tamil Poetry," *Studies in Religion,* vol. 3, pp. 205–19. Proponents of the later dates often ascribe the "songs," or lyrical passages, to earlier times. A comprehensive discussion of the dating is found in Marvin H. Pope, *Song of Songs: A New Translation with Introduction and Commentary,* The Anchor Bible (Garden City, NY: Doubleday, 1977), pp. 22–34.

2. Tosephta Sanhedrin 12:10, and Yadayim 3:5.

3. Pope, *Song of Songs,* pp. 145–53.

4. The Gedullat Mosheh exists, at this writing, only in an Arabic version. However, a description exists in Louis Ginzberg, *The Legends of the Jews,* trans. Henrietta Szold (Philadelphia: The Jewish Publication Society, 1979), pp. 304–9.

5. Gershom G. Scholem, *Major Trends in Jewish Mysticism* (New York: Schocken, 1941), p. 52. Also pp. 40–79.

6. *Modern Poetry of the Arab World,* trans. Abdullah al-Udhari (New York: Viking Penguin, 1986), p. 29.

7. *The Selected Poetry of Yehuda Amichai,* trans. Stephen Mitchell and Chana Bloch (New York: Harper and Row, 1986), p. 90.

8. Robert Graves, *The Song of Songs: Text and Commentary* (New York: Potter, 1973), p. 15.

9. Maimonides (Moses ben Maimon), *Mishnah Torah, I, The Book of Knowledge,* 10:3, "Laws Concerning Repentance."

May Swenson's Art of Wonder

Body my house
my horse my hound
what will I do
when you are fallen

Where will I sleep
How will I ride
What will I hunt . . .

Those lines from May Swenson's "Question" have enthralled me for years, and perhaps they always will. They are hypnotic, having the rhythmic pull of a chant, the tone of awe. They terrify with shocking awareness that my body is not the real me. They follow with insistent questions, "what will I do," "How will I ride," "What will I hunt," "Where can I go," all ironic because they cannot be answered, their chill increased by obsessive rhyme ("house," "horse," "hound," "hunt," "mount").

Some years after I first read the poem, I saw an early version, scribbled and crossed out, line after discarded line, its wonder absent. "Body" was the name of Swenson's dog, her "good bright dog," as he is referred to, briefly, in the final draft. In the first take, she had dwelled on the poignant but more limited subject of the dog's death. The poet's thrilling address to the body as the self's armor had been conceived of as a song to the dead animal.

That discovery, though daunting at first, did not trouble me for long. The poet was an endless reviser. Unexpectedly, in con-

---

This essay is a new version based on two earlier pieces. One of them appeared as "Grace Schulman on May Swenson" in *Poetry Speaks, Expanded,* edited by Elise Paschen and Rebekah Presson Mosby (Naperville, IL: Sourcebooks, 2007). The other was published as "Life's Miracles" in *American Poetry Review* (Sept.–Oct. 1994).

trast to the mysterious aura of her poems, her composition was methodical. She kept a file filled with drafts, handwritten and typed, of nearly everything she wrote, sometimes as many as twenty sheets per poem. She placed them in folders, dated, the first being the draft she retyped and sent to an editor.

Whether her subjects are commonplace or unfamiliar, she presents them with an urgency that builds their impact. Often her poems, like "Question," are pitched low, having the tone of chatty, intimate speech, and have, at the same time, the music of charms, spells, and ritual dances.

May Swenson is a poet of endless curiosity. Questions are the wellsprings of her art. She asks about simple things, such as "What is the worm doing/making its hole," and about principles such as "What / is it about, / the universe, / the universe about us stretching out?" or, considering the moon landing, "Dare we land upon a dream?" In her speculations and her close observations, she fulfills Marianne Moore's formula for the working artist: "Curiosity, observation, and a great deal of joy in the thing." In subject matter a poet who, like Donne, takes all of knowledge as her province, she is as comfortable with animals and flowers as she is with anti-matter, electronic sound, and DNA.

Some of her chosen forms incorporate questions, such as her ballad, "The Centaur": "Where have you been?" "Been riding." Another is the ancient riddle, a form that enables her to concentrate on the object without naming it. "The Surface," for example, has affinities to Dickinson's riddles, and to her wit: "First I saw the surface, / then I saw it flow, / then I saw the underneath," the poet begins, and gradually unravels the answer, the image of an eye. Swenson riddles in a quest to find a higher reality obscured by conventional names, and to fathom what is deepest within the self. By rejecting ready-made definitions that enlighten us, Swenson sees in the dark. In a poem with the arresting title of "God," she derides the ordinary labeling of things with its consequent reduction of greatness:

They said there was a	Thing
that could not	Change
They could not	Find
it so they	Named
it	God

Unnaming allows her to rename, in an effort to see things outside the context of common parlance. Continually the search is for a deeper meaning, the essence of the thing observed. In "Evolution," the first poem of her first book, she exclaims:

> beautiful each Shape
> to see
> wonderful each Thing
> to name
> here a stone
> there a tree
> here a river
> there a Flame . . .

May Swenson was born in 1913 in Logan, Utah, of a Mormon family, and educated at Utah State University. She was a New Yorker from 1936, and lived in Sea Cliff, New York, for twenty-three years before her death in Ocean View, Delaware, in 1989. In her lifetime, she published eleven books over three decades, nine of them poetry collections, from *Another Animal* (1954) to *In Other Words* (1987). Honored as she was during her lifetime, her books included only four hundred and fifty of the nine hundred poems she composed. After her death, as new poems and new books continued to appear, it became clear that her output was large and her stature is major.

Nature (1994), one of the posthumous books, contains some early poems, until then unpublished, whose dominant tone is awe: "Remain aghast at life," the poet resolves in "Earth Your Dancing Place," composed as early as 1936:

> Enter each day
> as upon a stage
> lighted and waiting
> for your step . . .

Swenson's wonder is the enchantment of "Manyone Flying" (1975), another of the poems that appear posthumously in *Nature*. Here, the poet, in the guise of a high-flying bird, considers the divisions between the individual and humanity:

                              Out on the edge,
    my maneuverings,   my wings, think
       they are free.   Flock, where do we
    fly? Are we Ones?   Or One, only?
if only One, not lonely   . . . being Manyone . . .
            but Who   are We? And Why?

With nothing less than pure wonder, Swenson considers the Statue of Liberty, Washington Square, the sight of land from a plane. In "A Watch," the poet recalls its repair in a shop where she "felt privileged but also pained to watch the operation." With gleaming word-play ("my ticker going lickety-split"), she regards the watch as it becomes, metaphorically, a patient undergoing surgery.

Her intellectual probing is accompanied by a passionate identification with her subjects. She is fascinated with technology, such as, miraculously, the first telephoto of the whole earth taken from above the moon, this last in "Orbiter 5 Shows How Earth Looks from the Moon." Cast in the shape of the earth photo, the poem is striking for language that fairly leaps out of its picture ("A woman in the earth. / A man in the moon."). Nature, especially, intrigues this poet: the lion's yearning, autumn's "bruise-reds." In "The Woods at Night," she sees "The binocular owl, / fastened to a limb / like a lantern / all night long."

The Love Poems of May Swenson (1991), surely the liveliest of the posthumous books, contains poems that illuminate the work as a whole. The poet who continually questions existence finds love at the source of the quest: existence depends on the other. The bridge between self and other is basic to the polarities, found throughout her work, of life and death, wildness and restraint, past and present, sun and moon, stone and flame. Although out of the fifty-five poems, *The Love Poems* contains only thirteen unpublished previously, as well as some familiar poems in altered forms, they occupy the full span of her career, having been composed between 1938 and 1987. And their appearance in one volume strengthens their impact.

The poems are outrageously sexual. Heightened sensations recall the Song of Songs: "thy breasts shall be as clusters of the

vine" (King James Version 7:8). Swenson conveys physical inti-
macies and shares sensual delights, as, for example, the "dark
wild honey,"

> Thick transparent amber
> you brought home,
> the sweet that burns.

The sheer beauty of the love poems raises the question of
why Swenson did not publish all of them during her lifetime.
Such exclusions usually have complex reasons, but it is a fair as-
sumption that the times demanded discretion. With public dis-
closure of homosexual love, careers could be ruined, the work
disregarded. Pearl Schwartz, Swenson's lover from 1948 to
about 1961, is reported to have said: "She chose not to make
clear what her [sexual] leanings were. . . . It was dangerous at
the time to be gay." The quotation appears in a recent essay
called "The Figure in the Tapestry" by Paul Swenson, May's
brother.

Vivid and moving, the love poems take in the intricacies of
human nature, the natural world, geography, and invention.
They are spoken low, seductive and sly, but with outcries such as:
"Burn radiant sex born scorpion need." In them, she regards
the human body in a way that enlarges the dread of its loss. The
best of them are poems of intense love between women, composed at a time when that genre was rare in poetry. Sadly, they
were written in the closet and published only after her death.
Their lesbian imagery is subtle, and brilliantly dramatized: "I
open to your dew, / beginning in the spring again . . ." ("Annual"); "I exist in your verdant garden . . . I unfurled in your
rich soil" ("You Are"). And this, from "Neither Wanting More":

> To feel your breast
> rise with a sigh
> to hold you mirrored
> in my eye
>
> Neither wanting more
> Neither asking why

I say love between women with qualifications, because of the poetry's aesthetic complexity. Swenson's tone embraces the full human drama. Her metaphors often are male or animal or flower. Nevertheless, the sexual love she dramatizes so brilliantly is Sapphic:

> We are released
> and flow into each other's cup
> Our two frail vials pierced
> drink each other up
> —"In Love Made Visible," 1946

The poet cries out in joy: "a rain of diamonds / in the mind" ("Love Is"); of pain: "Now heart, take up your desert; / this spring is cursed" ("Wild Water," 1938); and of yearning: "my body is a sharpened dart / of longing / coming toward you always" ("The Equilibrist," composed in the 1940s).

In a biography published in 1993, *The Wonderful Pen of May Swenson,* R. R. Knudson wisely observed, "For May, power was fear pushed back." So, too, many of the love poems, like primitive chants, derive their power from the expression of inner wildness as well as the immense effort to order it. "The School of Desire" (*The Cage of Spines,* 1958) captures the poet's energies at their strongest:

> Unloosed, unharnessed, turned back to the wild by
>   love,
> the ring you cantered round with forelock curled,
> the geometric music of this world
> dissolved and, in its place,
> alien as snow to tropic tigers, amphitheatric space,
> you will know the desert's freedom, wind and sun
> rough-currying your mane, the plenitude
> of strong caresses on your body nude.

Sexy though they are, the love poems also evoke the elusiveness of a world beyond the physical. In the grand design of an Elizabethan sonneteer, she writes of mutability: desire changes, the moment it is given form, to flame up and die.

Love, a reaction against the process of temporal decay, can enable flesh-bound companions at least to intuit spiritual value.

> In love are we set free
> Objective bone
> and flesh no longer insulate us
> to ourselves alone . . .
>
> —"In Love Made Visible"

The Love Poems are a stage in Swenson's incessant inquiry. Early and late, her intellectual probing is accompanied by passionate identification with objects, with technology, and, especially, with nature: the lion's yearning, the lamb's way, the deer's eye; recumbent stones, thighs of trees, horses whose colors are "like leaves or stones, / wealthy textures, / liquors of light." On the other hand, when human love is at stake, human sensibility replaces the unity with animals, as in the poem "Evolution":

> an Evolution strange
> two Tongues touch
> exchange
> a Feast unknown
> to stone
> or tree or beast . . .

As for her persistent questioning, it is laid to rest when the lovers lie content: "Because I don't know you / I love you" is one paradoxical admission.

The love poems do not question outright. Instead, they probe in subtler ways the reality of being, as in the poet's earlier efforts. To be alive is to depend on one's opposite: "As you are sun to me / O I am moon to you," cries the lover in "Facing." "They are like flame and ice / the elemental You and Me," begins "The Indivisible Incompatibles," a poem written in the 1940s. The lovers are "Not twin / but opposite / as my two hands are opposite," according to "Symmetrical Companion," another early poem, from 1948, that has for an ending, "Come release me / Without you I do not yet exist." Even more directly, the beloved asserts:

I dwell
in you
and so
I know
I am

no one
can be sure
by himself
of his own being . . .

And, more firmly, "because you believe I exist I exist" ("You Are").

Here the passion is metaphorical, though the details are concrete. The lovers of her poems, steamy though they are, also represent parts of a divided self. Their union, that blessed state in which opposites are conjoined, reveals essential being. Mooring in one's otherness allays unanswerable queries about life and death. Furthermore, the process of finding a hidden part of the self reveals a remote world beyond the tangible: "In love are we made visible . . . In love are we set free."

The title of her 1967 volume, *Half Sun Half Sleep,* announces that division of what May Swenson once called "the primitive bipolar suspension in which my poems often begin to form." Her theme of division is conveyed by many of her shaped poems, or those which contain visual as well as textual metaphors.

The shapes are engaging, but the poetry's power is in cadence. Her impact is in urgent speech and incantatory rhythms, the music of charms, spells, curses, ritual dances. Never does the typography, however intricate, supersede the cadence. As in primitive poetry, word and appearance are fused for a total effect.

As if to demonstrate subtly that the shaped poems have an auditory life of their own, May Swenson chose to read aloud many of her typographical poems in 1976 on a Caedmon recording, which could not, of course, exhibit the visual pattern to her listeners. One of the poems she read was "The Lightning," which she referred to as a pivotal poem in *Half Sun Half Sleep.* Of its typographical device, the visual metaphor, she commented: "As seen on the page, there is a streak of white space that runs diagonally through the body of the poem and this even splits some of the words." The poem celebrates speech, and the white streak creates meditative pauses in lines, indicating the gap between word and event, between experience and its realization in the poem:

The Lightning

The lightning waked me. It slid unde   r
my eyelid. A black book flipped ope   n
to an illuminated page. Then insta   ntly
shut. Words of destiny were being   uttered in the distance. If only I   could
make them out! . . . Next day, as I   lay
in the sun, a symbol for concei   ving the
universe was scratched on my e   yeball
But quickly its point eclipse   d, and
softened, in the scabbard of   my brain.

On a Caedmon recording of the 1970s, Swenson spoke of a poem whose title is, antithetically, "Untitled." She described the visual metaphor created by the typographical appearance on the page, noting that "two black crooked lines pass through the text as if to x it out. The bipolar words 'you,' 'me,' are in the center as if entangled where the two black lines cross." Here, the spaces are between words, and they designate a meditative, almost painful effort at speech. "I will be earth you be the flower . . . ," the poem begins, and the voice rises in passionate intensity as the lovers flail, boat and sea, earth and flood, desert and salt.

That struggle to speak is manifest again in "Fountains of Aix," a poem from the 1963 collection, *To Mix With Time.* In it, the word "water" is split fifteen times from its lines, and poured, in effect, down the side of one stanza:

A goddess is driving a chariot through   water.
Her reins and whips are tight white   water.
Bronze hoofs of horses wrangle with   water.

The streak of space separates the fountain's sculptures from the water spouting from their mouths. Here are dolphins and

lions and bulls, and "faces with mossy lips unlocked," all utter-
ing water, "their eyes mad / or patient or blind or astonished."
She builds a metaphor of the fluidity of utterance, and thence
of poetry. Swenson's pauses emphasize her wonder: In "Fire
Island," from *Iconographs* (1970), the poet contemplates the miracle of beholding light and dark—milky foam, black sky—of
solitude and the group—walkers on the beach and "other
watchers"—while the two ends of the narrow island are splayed
out in type above and below, creating pauses between the letters
of the words "fire" and "sight."

Typographical pauses appear throughout Swenson's writing
career. Some are part of an intricate pattern, as in "The Fountains of Aix" and "The Lightning." Many occur in poems of two
columns, and of those, some are read down the page, some
across the page and still others across and down. Early and late,
those patterned spaces between the words indicate opposites,
ironies, reversals, paradoxes, ambiguities. For example, in a
poem whose title conveys a moment in time, "While Sitting in
the Tuileries and Pacing the Slanting Sun," the poet ironically
associates, and then divides by space, a swaddled infant in
Giotto's fresco, "Birth of the Virgin," and a mummy in the Vatican Museum:

There is a	Person
of flesh that is a rocking	Box
There is a	Box
of wood that is a painted	Person . . .

In "Bleeding," from *Iconographs,* a space through the center is
a jagged, running wound, effecting caesuras of hesitation in a
dialogue between the knife and the cut. The force grows along
with the grim realization that bleeding is precisely feeling, in
this devastating relationship:

I feel I have to bleed to   feel I   think said the cut.
I don't I don't have to   feel said   the knife drying now
becoming shiny.

As the opposites throughout her work have their roots in the
love poems, so have the contrasts created by her typographical

separations. There are the two columns of "Evolution" and "Facing" (both to be read down the page, rather than across), each indicating another animal, the lover who is an aspect of the self. Like all the love poems, these two praise opposite beings—flame and ice, sun and moon—who move forward to their destiny.

Swenson's love poems, with their high energy and "desert freedom," are ironic in showing that vitality can emphasize its very opposite, life's decline. From early on, May Swenson sings of life in death's shadow, as in "Question," quoted above, and in poems that have the word "Death" in their titles: "Deaths," "Death Invited," "The Shape of Death."

Did Swenson suffer great personal loss? Her biographer, R. R. Knudson, writes that the death of a beloved grandfather prompted May, as a child, to question the finality of loss. Then, as a teenager, May questioned Mormonism, and, in fact, normative religions with their conventional notions of God. It seems that later she was deeply saddened by the atrocities of World War II. Young May's lover, the Czech poet, Anca Vrboska, lost her family to the Nazi death camps. While Vrboska wrote of Auschwitz directly, Swenson internalized, objectified, searched, as always, for the essence of death:

> I will lie down in autumn
> let birds be flying
>
> Swept into a hollow
> by the wind
> I'll wait for dying
>
> I will lie inert unseen
> my hair same-colored
> with grass and leaves . . .
>> —"I Will Lie Down"

Later still, in those poems whose titles say "death," Swenson plays on the Elizabethan paradox that tragic implications are perceived in the midst of life's personal, intimate experience. All are poems that embody contrasts, either in their divided shape on the page, or in their imagery, or both. A fascinating early example is "Death, Great Smoothener":

                    Death,
               great smoothener,
               maker of order,
      arrester, unraveler, sifter and changer;
            death, great hoarder;
       student, stranger, drifter, traveler,
     flyer and nester all caught at your border;
                    death,
                great halter;
         blackener and frightener,
            reducer, dissolver,
     seizer and welder of younger with elder,
              waker with sleeper,
            death, great keeper
            of all that must alter;
                    death,
              great heightener,
              leaper, evolver,
            greater smoothener,
              great whitener!

Sheer energy cries life even as she speaks to death. The poem is a pagan incantation, with its frightening direct address presented in clusters of heavy stresses, its falling rhythm, its depiction of death in lists of epithets, enforced by rhyme: "order," "hoarder," "border." In contrast to the chant rhythm, the typographical shape on the page is that of an ornate Christian cross. In the manner of Caedmon, the first English poet, who sang of God's Creation using pagan Anglo-Saxon epithets ("keeper," "ruler"), Swenson, chanting death in life, contrasts the pagan rhythm with the shape of a Christian cross.

The poetry of May Swenson celebrates life's miracles even with death in view: the wonder of speech ("Fountains of Aix"); the grandeur of God ("God"); the radiance of sight ("Fire Island"). In each of these three poems, typographical divisions—white streaks down the middle of the text—make for breath-catching pauses that enhance the excited tone. The ambiguities and paradoxes of Swenson's poetry result from the basic contradiction between our illusion of permanence and our underlying certainty of fatality. This contradiction is articulated most explicitly in one of the love poems, "The Shape of Death."

What does love look like? We know the shape of death.
Death is a cloud, immense   and awesome. At first a
lid is lifted from the   eye of light. There is a
clap of sound. A white   blossom belches from the
jaw of fright.

Swenson is intimate with death, as she is with life and with love. She is at her most intimate, though, with the natural world. "At Truro" finds the poet so close to the sea as to read her own biography in the encroaching waves. She sees herself as a crab, a coral, a sea worm, until, caught like a fish to dry on land, she strikes a dark note: "In brightness I lost track / of my underworld / of ultraviolet wisdom." But the sea remains in her, as we learn at the poem's startling conclusion: "As if the sun were blind / again I feel the suck / of the sea's dark mind." Like other poems, this one compels, haunts, surprises, catches us unaware. Swenson is at once a magician, a shaman, an intelligent companion.

Eliot's "Marina"
The Poet and the Designer

In "Marina," which was published in London when Eliot was forty-two, the poet writes of a man who achieves spiritual renewal after he has recovered a daughter who evokes a pure vision of beauty. The poem is illuminated by a letter written to E. McKnight Kauffer, the designer who was to illustrate the Ariel edition that appeared in 1930. By the time Eliot wrote the letter, dated July 24, 1930, each had expressed admiration for the other's work: Kauffer had written to congratulate Eliot on "For Lancelot Andrewes" (1928), and, in this letter, Eliot praises Kauffer's illustrations. About "Marina," his new poem, he confides:

> The theme is paternity; with a crisscross between the text and the quotation. The theme is a comment on the Recognition Motive in Shakespeare's later plays, and particularly of course the recognition of Pericles. The quotation is from "Hercules Furens", where Hercules, having killed his children in a fit of madness induced by an angry god, comes to without remembering what he has done. (I didnt give the reference for fear it might be more distracting than helpful to the reader who did not grasp the exact point): the contrast of death and life in Hercules and Pericles.

The story behind the Ariels is compelling. The friendship of Eliot and E[dward] McKnight Kauffer began in the mid-1920s,

---

This is a new version based on two earlier pieces. One is an unpublished "Memorial Lecture" to The T. S. Eliot Society, St. Louis, Missouri, September 26, 2008. The other is "Notes on the Theme of 'Marina' by T. S. Eliot" in *Essays from the Southern Review,* edited by James Olney (Oxford: Clarendon Press, 1988).

both of them expatriates in London, and lasted until the artist's death in 1954. Aside from their shared respect for each other's work, the two men had a physical resemblance, both willowy with aquiline profiles, and addressed each other as "Bro." for "Brother" or "Missouri" and "Montana," after their home states. Eliot was born in St. Louis two years before Kauffer's birth in Great Falls, Montana, in 1890. In Eliot's letters to Kauffer, he becomes a whimsical, affectionate friend. In 1951, signing as "Missouri," Eliot asks, "Did you know that more poets come from Missouri than any other state in the Union?" In the early letter about his beautiful "Marina," he seems especially vulnerable: "I hope you like it: I don't know whether it is any good at all," and tells Kauffer: "Yours are the only decorations I can endure." Within a later message, a formal endorsement of Kauffer's work for a show in 1949, there is a caring aside to the artist then in America, imploring him to return to London, where he has a place "in the hearts of friends."

Aside from "Marina," Kauffer also designed and illustrated the separate editions of "Journey of the Magi" (1927), "A Song for Simeon" (1928), and "Triumphal March" (1931), actually one of the Ariels but placed as one of the *Coriolan* "Unfinished Poems" in Eliot's *Collected Poems*. Various authors are listed elsewhere in the Ariel series, their single poems published in pamphlets by Faber & Gwyr, later Faber & Faber. Eliot liked the title "Ariel," with its shades of Shakespeare and Laforgue, and he kept it in his *Collected Poems*. The four editions were given to me by the artist, a man I called Uncle Ted, who had become a friend of my parents, Bernard and Marcella Waldman, when he returned to America in 1940. He also gave me the letter with a copy of the typescript of "Marina."

Kauffer, a celebrated designer in London, had come to New York looking for work. My father, an advertising executive who had admired Kauffer's work, commissioned an airlines poster immediately after they met. Both shared the belief that no conflict exists between fine art and graphic design.

While the daughter image in "Marina" has its roots in Eliot's imagination, as well as in his allusions, Kauffer had an actual daughter, Ann, who lived in England until her death in 1996. Not the least of Kauffer's reasons for his attachment to me was that his daughter and I were, roughly, contemporaries. When Kauffer moved to America at the outset of World War II, Ann remained in England with her mother, Grace Ehrlich Kauffer. He was never to see Ann again.

Shortly after Kauffer's death, my own father met Kauffer's daughter, Ann, at an exhibition of Kauffer's posters in the Geffrye Museum, an outpost of the Victoria and Albert Museum in East London. There began a friendship between Ann and me, Kauffer's real daughter and his daughter's counterpart, that existed until her death.

Kauffer's Ariel illustrations are fired by early twentieth-century techniques, revolutionary in their time, particularly Cubism and Vorticism. He was fascinated, too, with science, especially geometry. "We live in an age of T-Squares and compasses," he wrote, and he disciplined his art with circles and squares, geometric pattern designs and the rectilinear line. In the 1920s, as a painter, Kauffer had been a member of the London Group, a society of painters influenced by Cubism. As a graphics designer, he used Cubist techniques in his posters, beginning with four gouaches for the London Underground Railways, and designed fine editions, such as Robert Burton's *Anatomy of Melancholy,* for Frances Meynall's Nonesuch Press. In 1916 in London, Kauffer saw the first exhibit of the Vorticists, whose work caught his feeling for the energy of the diagonal and for speed as a metaphor for the Machine Age. Diagonal rain and lightning flashes enliven his work, and in the Ariel "Marina" diagonals are juxtaposed with ovals. The magic of Eliot's poetry is manifold, but much of it has to do with contrasts: dingy words and large abstractions; visions and revisions. Kauffer's contrasts of oval and line are especially suited to "Marina," with its oppositions of death and life, and of past and present: allusions signify the past, and the present moment is set forth intensely and movingly by the modern speaker.

Kauffer's illustration for the Ariel edition shows no feminine image. It is a drawing of a starlit sea in the background and a double image of man in the foreground, apparently Pericles and the modern speaker rising from him. It is fitting, for "Marina" is not a persona poem. Although the speaker is unified with Pericles and with *Hercules Furens,* neither speaks for him. Both are friendly allusions, of deeds and thoughts analogous to the modern man. With rejuvenated vision, he attains wholeness, and rejects what only *seems* to be life for a life beyond the present moment. And later, in the *Quartets,* Eliot uses a modern speaker, without persona and without the guidance of figures from the past with shared actions that are central to the narratives.

The image was not the first to enter the designer's mind. In a letter dated July 29, 1930, Kauffer wrote to Eliot that the words "give, sympathise, control," as they appear in *The Waste Land* (1922), as well as the phrase "freeing of the waters," had run through his mind constantly, and, in fact, had been the central theme of a first illustration idea for "Marina." Undoubtedly, though, he saw the water imagery as a reversal of the barren despair of the earlier poem.

Some comments in Eliot's letter are clues to the poet's joyful vision in "Marina." Like the recognition scene in Shakespeare's *Pericles,* the poet's "recognition" in "Marina" of life's renewal comes about at sea, or at least in shallow waters. The epigraph from *Hercules Furens* is *Quis hic locus, quae regio, quae mundi plaga?*

"Marina" begins ironically in the rhythm of the epigraph, but the speaker's joy is antithetical to the horror that Hercules has killed those he loves:

> What seas what shores what grey rocks and what islands
> What water lapping the bow
> And scent of pine and the woodthrush singing through
> > > the fog
> O my daughter.*

---

* In the typescript of "Marina" that Eliot sent to Kauffer, the first stanza ended: "What images return / And reform around—O my daughter." The words "And reform around—" were deleted in printed editions. Also, what appeared in published versions as the third, fourth, and fifth stanzas are joined in the typescript. In these lines of the typescript, the words "The forms reform" appear, and are excluded from printed versions: "Whispers and small laughter between leaves and hurrying feet / Under sleep, where all the waters meet / The forms reform." Indentations of first lines appear in "Marina," which is in *The Complete Poems and Plays* (New York, 1952), 72–73, and is quoted in this text.

Death images crowd a chant in the second stanza: "Those who sharpen the tooth of the Dog, meaning / Death." In the third, they "are become insubstancial [*sic*], reduced by a wind." The speaker awakens in these marvelous lines:

> What is this face, less clear and clearer,
> The pulse in the arm, less strong and stronger—
> Given or lent? more distant than stars and nearer than
> the eye . . .

And, at the climax of the poem, the speaker declares:

> This form, this face, this life
> Living to live in a world of time beyond me; let me
> Resign my life for this life, my speech for that
> unspoken,
> The awakened, lips parted, the hope, the new ships.

Eliot's attraction to the "Recognition Motive," as he calls it in the letter, occurs elsewhere in his prose. In his essay, "John Ford," Eliot asserts that the father-daughter recognitions in Shakespeare's late plays, Perdita, Marina, and Miranda, "share some beauty of which his earlier heroines do not possess the secret." In *Pericles*, also set by the sea, the king fears death from joy in finding his lost daughter "Call'd Marina / For I was born at sea." In finding her, he cries:

> Down on thy knees, thank the holy gods as loud
> as thunder threatens us: this is Marina.
>
> (v.i. 200–201)

Instead of dying, Pericles is born again in the fusion of his life with hers.

But the Pericles allusion never becomes a persona. Finding his daughter, Pericles cries out: "O, come hither, / Thou that beget'st him that did thee beget . . ." United, they remain separate beings. On the other hand, in Eliot's "Marina," the startling rediscovery leads to a full realization of self, fuller, in fact, than that of any Ariel persona. It comes about gradually. Then:

I have made this, I have forgotten
And remember.
The rigging weak and the canvas rotten
Between one June and another September.
Made this unknowing, half conscious, unknown, my own.

The motion of images "forming and re-forming" (a phrase used in the earlier version) around his daughter is completed in the final unification:

What seas what shores what granite islands toward my timbers
And woodthrush calling through the fog
My daughter.

Those beautiful lines command utter silence. Still, I'll say that in *Ash Wednesday*, which was published a few months before "Marina," there is also the sea and shore, the quest for the unspoken word, and the theme of dying into life, which asks for the denial of all things in the hope of renewal. In "Marina," though, the sea is less accessible, the sea smell lost. Also, the end is in view, with the resignation of old life for new. What is more, the rewards are more immediately apparent: by stanza three, the death-rites of life without the experience of a higher reality are put to rest, "dissolved in place" by the liberating power of the recovered daughter. And Eliot's allusions to Hercules and Pericles enable the modern speaker to awaken with more clarity and ease than the protagonist of *Ash Wednesday*. In "Marina," motion of images re-forming around the daughter is completed in the final words, "My daughter."

The speaker's complex emotions in "Marina"—baffled, bemused, unendingly grateful—arise from a deeply personal "detachment" here and elsewhere in Eliot's poetry. The poem is best read that way, standing alone and without additional background. Still, that reading was affirmed for me by Ted Kauffer's letters, which tell of the Kauffer-Eliot friendship. In them I encountered an empathetic, patient, affectionate side of Eliot I had guessed at but not known, a different man from the one I had perceived.

After Kauffer died, my father visited T. S. Eliot in London, and spoke of their friend's last illness and death. He told him he had bent over Kauffer's bed at Lenox Hill Hospital, and, close to his ear, whispered "Montana," the nickname given him by "Missouri" Eliot. At that moment, Kauffer rallied, but, some days later, he sank back into a coma and died. One detail, one brief gesture, of Eliot's response captured the man entirely. He told me that Eliot, hearing the story about the friend he had encouraged and praised since the late 1920s, removed a white handkerchief meticulously placed to protrude one-quarter of an inch above his pocket. Slowly, deliberately, he dabbed a real tear from his eye. Then he replaced the handkerchief, exactly as it had been.

Marianne Moore

The Mind and the World

To read a poem by Marianne Moore is to be aware of exactitude. It is to know that the writer has looked at a subject—a cliff, a sea animal, an ostrich—from all sides, and has examined the person looking at it as well. For this poet, seeing an object meant speaking of its various aspects on many levels of discourse, and she created rhetorical debates that ranged from simple conversations (as in "I May, I Might, I Must") to dialectical arguments (as in "Critics and Connoisseurs") to complex inner arguments (as in "The Paper Nautilus" and "No Swan So Fine"). Actually, that argumentation propels the poems forward and turns our attention to their progress from beginning to end. In fact, the process through which the poems come to terms with the world is fundamental, for the aesthetic elements of the poems constitute their form for engagement with larger issues.

The poems of Marianne Moore, with their precise, compact renderings of objects and animals, are concerned with such matters as the courage to endure under brutal pressure; the ordinary virtues of patience and tenacity; and the endeavor to maintain personal integrity in a world of fragmentation. To explore these matters the poet enacts the struggle of the heart and mind to see the realities of this world as well as "the genuine," or the truths of an ideal realm.

The permanence of Marianne Moore's poetry is in its depiction of a dramatic struggle between the poet's mind and the

First published in *Poetry Pilot,* Academy of American Poets, November 1984.

world. Objects and animals embody the mind's tenacious, life-giving power that

> tears off the veil; tears
> the temptation, the
> mist the heart wears,
>> from its eyes—if the heart
>> has a face
>> —"The Mind Is an Enchanting Thing"

In each of the poems, the mind, engaged with an object or animal, moves forward to a fresh, startling idea. In "The Paper Nautilus," the speaker, contemplating the sea animal taking care of her eggs, works through to the idea of love as "the only fortress / strong enough to trust to." The notion is at once parallel and antithetical to the "entrapped writers" and the authorities at the outset of the poem, since we find in each statement about the nautilus a reference to the limited people. In this way, the mind, exploring everything about an object, has seen beyond it to the world.

Her poetics is rooted in the native "instinct to amass and reiterate" that she ascribed to her countryman in an essay, "Henry James as a Characteristic American." Although her approach to subject matter changed throughout her career, she chose essentially the same kinds of material, which included elephants she had seen in a lecture-film on Ceylon, an icosasphere she had read about in *The New York Times*, a lyrebird she had seen in an engraving by Thomas Bewick, an exhibit of sixteenth-century Persian treasures. Her poetry carries forward the American tradition in its use of the commonplace, and in its insistence on the poet's freedom to contemplate any subject without diminished energy: Being an American was for her, as she wrote of Henry James, "intrinsically and actively ample, . . . reaching westward, southward, anywhere, everywhere," with a mind "incapable of the shut door in any direction."

Hers is a poetry of facts, science, and common lives. And for her, to feel passion is to see clearly: Perception affirms the endeavor of the veiled heart, the confounded mind, and the eye that cannot easily see beyond conventional surfaces, to come to terms with the truth of existence in the modern world. Under her inquiring gaze are the wonder of modern love ("Marriage"), the proliferation of sights and sounds that crowd the senses ("Those Various Scalpels"), the vast, puzzling structure of the urban metropolis ("People's Surroundings"), and the unity that each person strives for in a life that urges disruption. Beyond that, she ventures to apprehend permanent truths that are seen by the eye of the mind.

Central to her poetry of the mind's inward growth is her use of metamorphic imagery that accentuates the tendency of consciousness to pivot continuously from one vivid figure to another. Her vision of a shifting reality is a further indication of her sense of the age, whose leading philosophers have questioned the accuracy of objective reality. "What is more precise than precision? Illusion," exclaims the speaker, upholding the twentieth-century view that what we perceive to be real is not actual, and that optical illusion is the rule, rather than the exception.

Metamorphic images, then, are used to embody the shifting process of the mind in its encounter with modern reality. Metamorphosis is the function of the poet, who creates what is real by defining it in terms of changes he perceives. To elucidate this process of change, Marianne Moore does not rely on standard metamorphic myths such as Daphne, Proteus, or Ariel, but on objects from the world around her that move as they are perceived. Images of water, fire, and rock—those classic elements of metamorphosis—abound in her poetry, often accompanying moments of change. Other instances are images that are dialectical in that they move and are moved, act and are acted upon, see and are seen ("enchanting"/"enchanted," "enslaver"/"enslaved"). Those images, and the ways in which they are moved for the effect of magical change, enact the struggle of consciousness toward illumination.

In Marianne Moore's poetry, creativity rises from the subtle dialectic between freedom and repression. We learn of the camel-sparrow's struggle for freedom in "He 'Digesteth Harde Yron'," from Hercules, who was "hindered to succeed" in "The Paper Nautilus," from the salamander in "His Shield" who knows that freedom is "the power of relinquishing / what one would keep."

In her poetry, freedom is built on the very limitations that life imposes. Just as the poet's fascination with worldly things is generated by life's boundaries, her concept of freedom is that liberty which is won despite the laws of constraint. In an essay called "Idiosyncrasy and Technique," she wrote of the artistic process: "Creative secrets, are they secrets? Impassioned interest in life, that burns its bridges behind it and will not contemplate defeat, is one, I would say."

And her meditative poem, "What Are Years," deals with a restricted freedom that is, paradoxically, the source of creative energy. That aesthetic is, I believe, at the heart of the poetry of Marianne Moore:

He

> Sees deep and is glad, who
> accedes to mortality
> and in his imprisonment rises
> upon himself as
> the sea in a chasm, struggling to be
> free and unable to be,
>> in its surrendering
>> finds its continuing.

First Loves

The first poem I fell in love with was in a language I did not understand. At bedtime my father declaimed—that is, chanted from memory—"The Romantic," by Adam Mickiewicz, in his native Polish, which he tried to teach me and thought I comprehended. Although I missed nearly every word of the long ballad, I heard in his voice bells, arias, the sound of a clarinet's low notes. My father had been educated in London and New York, but his voice was never as vibrant as when he recited Mickiewicz, the poet of his youth. During recitations, his eyes widened and his hands described arcs that summoned demons and trolls. When my American grandfather plied me with Longfellow's "Hiawatha" and Abraham Lincoln's speeches, I was soothed by familiar meanings, but I quietly longed for my father's enactment of "The Romantic."

One of many reasons I regret not having learned Polish is that the work of Mickiewicz, a nineteenth-century poet once revered in his native land, has not been translated widely. Still, I found "The Romantic" years later in an English version by W. H. Auden, quoted by Czeslaw Milosz in his remarkable memoir, *The Land of Ulro*. The ballad is of a woman who believes she sees her love two years after his death and burial. When a villager derides her vision, the poet, in the role of a wandering stranger, joins the crowd in supporting her, exclaiming: "Cold eye, look in your heart." To my dismay, the poem no longer had the magic of the words whose meanings escaped me. But my father's voice—rough, emotive, musical—awakened me to poetry. From that time on, I looked for the secrets locked in words.

Originally appeared in *First Loves*, edited by Carmela Cuirara (New York: Scribner's, 2000).

My father's recitations led me to my real first love, from which I have never strayed. It is another ballad, coincidentally written by the translator of the earlier poem: Auden's "The Quarry," its title changed in his *Collected Poems* to "O What Is That Sound." On a lucky birthday morning, my parents gave me "Pleasure Dome," edited by Lloyd Frankenberg, an LP record album, and a portable phonograph to play it on. I was startled to hear Auden reading from his work, in company with Elizabeth Bishop, Marianne Moore, T. S. Eliot, and Dylan Thomas.

Startled, yes. The poet recited his lines in an age that preceded large poetry readings, tapes of *The Iliad* playing on automobile cassettes, and CDs holding volumes of spoken words. Only on rare occasions would a celebrated poet read at the Y or at the Frick museum. But my record spun for me and, occasionally, for a keen friend. The album required care. I had to watch the needle's fall, making sure it didn't cut across grooves. I dusted the record by toweling it gently while it spun. All that year, "Pleasure Dome" was my Xanadu and I was Kubla Khan.

When I heard Auden render the first words of his ballad, "O What Is That Sound," I shuddered in fear. His voice, clipped and tranquil, presented characters who barely control their mounting frenzy:

> O what is that sound which so thrills the ear
> Down in the valley drumming, drumming?
> Only the scarlet soldiers, dear,
> The soldiers coming.

As I read the poem now, the image of "the soldiers coming" is never specified. The soldiers are symbols of an apparently harmless but potential force grown real. The ballad unfolds in the tense dialogue of an anxious couple, one of them questioning, the other feigning calm. The details are vivid, provided by the strained questioner, the wary answerer: "scarlet soldiers," "sun on their weapons," "all that gear," the parson's "white hair." However clear, though, the images do not illuminate the developing catastrophe. Even as the soldiers come closer, the central situation is a mystery. Just who the soldiers are, and why they are coming, are unanswered questions.

In each quatrain, the fear heightens. Complex emotions range from apprehension ("O what is that light") to transparent attempts at comfort ("only the sun") to flat denial ("O it must be the farmer") to flight ("I must be leaving") to disaster ("splintered the door").

When I first read "The Quarry," I linked its form to the dramatic story-songs I'd heard as a child:

> Who killed Cock Robin?
> I said the sparrow,
> With my bow and arrow,
> I killed Cock Robin.

Often the traditional ballads, built on a single event, begin with lines that suggest imminent danger:

> There was a great ship sailing in the North Country
> And the name of the ship was the Golden Vanity
> And they feared she might be taken by the Turkish enemy
> That sailed upon the lowland, lowland, lowland,
> That sailed upon the lowland sea.

Remembering them now, I marvel that despite their scant settings, absent motives, and want of crucial details, irrelevant details are supplied in abundance, often with numbers. In "The Demon Lover," for example, the devil coming to claim a married young matron boasts of his "seven ships" and his "four-and-twenty bold mariners," and persuades her to leave her "two babes." In "O What Is That Sound" Auden builds on the traditional ballad, boldly using the question and answer narrative, the details that, though clear, never disclose the reason for distress. At the same time, his characters are complex, intriguing, real. "The soldiers coming" pursue us all.

Very recently I read in Edward Mendelson's splendid biography, *The Later Auden*, that nearly forty years after he wrote the poem, Auden revealed its inspiration: a painting of Christ's Agony in the Garden (probably by Bellini) with soldiers crossing a bridge. "Visually they look quite harmless and there is nothing to show whither they are going. It is only because one has read the Gospel story that one knows that, in fact, they are coming to arrest Jesus." He added: "I have never dreamed of being pursued by soldiers, and I don't know if others have, but . . . it seemed reasonable to me that they could function for all readers as a symbol."

In my early reading of the ballad, Auden's troops forecast doom, his, mine, everyone's. While I know that world events had only a minor role in the poem's impact on me, I will recall them nevertheless: I had been a child of World War II, an American Jew haunted by news of Nazi brutality in Europe. Over and again I dreamed of soldiers in black uniforms shouldering rifles when I tried to escape from a barricaded city. One afternoon I saw American soldiers at rest, presumably on leave, harmlessly lolling about Central Park. I remember thinking "soldiers at rest" and then of the pun, "soldiers arrest." But now as then I know that Auden's soldiers transcend personal fears. They bode terror for everyone, regardless of time, place, or circumstance.

My love for poetry began in mystery, from my father's Polish recitations to folk ballads to Auden's "The Quarry," that first version of "O What Is That Sound." It rooted in fear of the unknown and in the challenge of silences. As a poet I find mystery to be vital still, running only a close second to praise, and perhaps the two are linked in expressions of awe. I think of Auden: "Teach the free man how to praise." Rilke: "Ich rühme." Hopkins: "He fathers-forth whose beauty is past change: Praise him." But that is a story for another time.

The Persistence of Tradition

Tradition has a way of exerting its strongest hold on us when we are least aware of its presence. At times an unfamiliar genre—the Mayan legend, the Swahili wedding song—affects us so profoundly that we bear its traces without giving it a name. Harold Bloom writes of that tendency in *Agon: Towards a Theory of Revisionism*. He states: "Unnaming always has been a major mode in poetry, far more than naming; perhaps there cannot be a poetic naming that is not founded on an unnaming."[1]

The process of unnaming intrigues me, for many deep sympathies have no apparent explanation. Recently I finished writing a poem called "Footsteps on Lower Broadway," in which I identified closely with three nineteenth-century figures: Henry James, Walt Whitman, and my grandfather, a Hungarian-born Jewish immigrant. What bonded the unlikely trio for me were their separate but similar predilections for lower New York. At different times, Whitman and my grandfather saw Grace Church steeple as they walked up from the Battery, listened to Italian opera, and heard street shouts of merchants and reformers. Henry James and my grandfather saw the tall buildings I pass by every day, some of them decorated with stone gargoyles, animals, and griffins.

Since writing the poem, a ballade of ten ten-line stanzas, I have thought continually about the mysterious nature of handing down. Apart from my affinities for language and for walking in lower New York, I cannot classify the enormous impact those men have had on my life and work.

Originally appeared in *Where We Stand,* edited by Sharon Bryan (New York: W. W. Norton, 1994). Reprinted from *River City,* 13, no. 2 (Spring 1993).

What intrigues me, though, is the attractions James and Whitman had to the heritage of my grandfather, a man they never knew. For James, that interest is conveyed less in the content than in the vigorous tone of his language. In *The American Scene*, James writes of viewing, at the age of sixty-two, the Lower East Side ghetto of European immigrant Jews. My grandfather had moved away years before, first to attend law school and then to establish a practice on lower Broadway. Noting the crowded living conditions, James was appalled but fascinated. He used excited words such as "bristled" and "swarmed." He wrote: "The scene hummed with the human presence beyond any I have ever faced."[2]

For Whitman, the appeal was overwhelming. In March 1842, Whitman, at twenty-three, attended services twice at a synagogue in lower Manhattan, and reported his experiences in leaders he wrote for his newspaper, *The Aurora*. He visited the Shearith Israel Synagogue on Crosby Street, a modest building dwarfed by St. Paul's nearby. Whitman's account is worth quoting at length, for it is filled with wonder so intense as to show him at a loss for words. The poet who was born of Dutch and English farm folk with Quaker tendencies was new to Jewish ritual. He was dazzled by the ancient forms of worship and by the chants, the more so because he did not comprehend the strange language. His lack of comprehension led to a narrative mode that was simultaneously halting *and* urgent. He wrote:

> The whole scene was entirely new; never had we beheld any
> thing of a similar description before. The congregation
> (we don't know what other word to use) were all standing,
> each one with his hat on. . . . In the middle of the room
> was a raised platform about four yards square, with heavy
> balustrade of bronze work and mahogany around it. Upon
> the centre of this platform was a figure which, by the voice
> coming from it, we knew to be a man. None of the linea-
> ments of the human form, however, were visible; for one of
> the large silk mantles alluded to was thrown over his head,
> and completely shrouded him. He was speaking; but as his
> language was Hebrew, we could not understand a word he
> uttered.[3]

Unable to define, or even to name, the sacred Ark that holds the Torah (five books of Moses), Whitman marveled at its part in the service:

At the further end of the room stood an erection very much resembling the front that pictures give the ancient Parthenon. Under it was a semicircular partitioned enclosure, of panelled wood, which from the ornaments and expensive tracery lavished upon the whole affair seemed intended to contain something either very valuable, or very sacred.

It was the Ark he returned to in his second account, again in the tone of uninitiated enchantment, unknowing, unnaming:

After the performance had continued for some time as we described it in yesterday's *Aurora*, some of the Jews went up to the semicircular panel work before mentioned, unlocked it, and opened the doors. Three or four of them took from the inclosure certain contrivances, which we dare hardly pretend to describe, for fear of bungling in the attempt. As near as we can now recollect, they resembled in shape large sugar loaves; and each had an ornamental and fantastic affair made of silver and glass upon its top. These were brought up to the platform in the centre, and each of the silver ornaments we have described was taken from the top of the sugar loaf structure, and put upon the desk in front. The priest then raised aloft a large scroll of parchment, probably the sacred law—wafting it around so that the people could see it in all parts of the house. All this while he uttered a kind of chant, to which the men and women made responses.

Lacking names, Whitman focused on the imagery, the rhythms, the human involvement. He was transported:

The heart within us felt awed as in the presence of memorials from an age that had passed away centuries ago. The strange and discordant tongue—the mystery, and all the associations that crowded themselves in troops upon our mind—made a thrilling sensation to creep through every nerve. It was indeed a sight well calculated to impress the mind with an unwonted tone.

Enchanted as he was, Whitman did not use the ritual as a topic in his poetry. In his verse, there are no references to the synagogue services and only cursory allusions to Hebrew music. That in itself is not more surprising than any poet's omission of an exciting experience. However, it does seem odd that in his great passage concerning world religions, Judaism does not appear. The section beginning "I do not despise you, priests" (*Leaves of Grass,* Chant 43) includes the priest, the lama, and the Brahmin, but not the rabbi. And although the Koran and the Gospels are named among the poet's scriptures, the Torah— "the ornamental and fantastic affair" that had charmed him years before—is not.

Nor would the lapse of thirteen years between the *Aurora* leaders and the first publication of *Leaves of Grass* explain the omission of Judaism from the poetry. Whitman incorporated much that was contemporaneous with the synagogue ritual: the contralto in the organ loft, the omnibus drivers, "the blab of the pave," "the vault at Pfaff's." And even if, in the interim, he was attracted far more to other Eastern philosophies, he was a poet who gathered in and contained ideas simultaneously, rather than moving from one to another.

From the newspaper account, I would surmise that his exclusion had to do with the impossibility of examining what he could not name. The poet who wrote "all truths wait in things" studied identifiable objects that embodied the spirit. In the Jewish services he found truths without things he could identify. It might have been equivalent to the unearthly "journeywork of the stars" without its earthly equivalent, the "leaves of grass" drawing the mind toward the celestial.

Actually, Judaism is fundamental to Whitman's verse but in a more subtle way. A clue to the poet's practice is in his prose, a later (1888) essay called "The Bible as Poetry," first collected in *November Boughs.* Here he lauds the Hebrew poets for their bold figurative language and their concerns with vital emotions:

The metaphors daring beyond account, the lawless soul, extravagant by our standards, the glow of love and friendship, the fervent kiss—nothing in argument or logic, but unsurpass'd in proverbs, in religious ecstasy, in suggestions of common mortality and death, man's great equalizers—the spirit everything, the ceremonies and forms of the churches nothing, faith limitless, its immense sensuousness immensely spiritual—an incredible, all-inclusive non-worldliness and dew-scented illiteracy (the antipodes of our Nineteenth Century business absorption and morbid refinement)—no hair-splitting doubts, no sickly sulking and sniffling, no "Hamlet," no "Adonais," no "Thanatopsis," no "In Memoriam."[4]

What Whitman said he admired in Hebrew poetry he had consecrated in his own verse years before. "Logic and sermons do not convince," he asserts in *Leaves of Grass,* just as, throughout his verse, he celebrates the spirit and its companion, sensuousness, over the church.

More significant, though, is his musical affinity to the Hebrew Bible. In his biography, *Walt Whitman: A Life,* Justin Kaplan writes that in the poet's religious education at St. Ann's Episcopal and at the Dutch Reformed Church, "he was duly instructed in Scripture and catechism, but what remained with him was the Bible's rhythm and imagery. . . ."[5] The magnificent long sentence quoted above from Whitman's essay, "The Bible as Poetry," is in an acervate style, its amassment and reiteration of detail focusing attention on the writer's process of thought. That manner of listing is prominent in the Hebrew Bible as well as in Whitman's poetry.

And, of course, Whitman follows the Hebrew Bible in his recurrent uses of anaphora:

> All spheres, grown, ungrown, small, large, suns, moons, planets,
> All distances of place however wide,
> All distances of time, all inanimate forms . . .

and parallelism:

> Forests at the bottom of the sea, the branches and leaves . . .
> —Both passages from "Sea-Drift"

And besides the poetic devices, entire structural concepts from the Hebrew Bible made their way into Whitman's verse. The rhythmic divisions of the Song of Songs, whose chapters are sequences of verse modulated from theme to theme, one image suggesting another, are analogous to the chants in *Leaves of Grass*.

What the poet was unable to identify he was unable to exclude. Whitman's youthful fondness for biblical rhythm was sharpened by the odd synagogue chants in the "strange and discordant tongue," the music that was to inform his own.

As it was with Whitman, it is with us all. We are carriers of images from countless cultures, some of which are unknown to us, some seemingly remote. Only in part are we shaped by writers we acclaim, for influences live in the unconscious. There are, in fact, mysterious transmissions of information between cultures that are far apart in time and space. The late Willard Trask, a major translator, offers an example: he observes that medieval Galician and Portuguese poets cultivated a genre called "the girl's song" that was similar in form—rhyme scheme, meter, and line recurrences—to songs in China of the sixth century B.C.E.[6] We know from "Songs of Cifar," the modern Nicaraguan epic by Pablo Antonio Cuadra, that folklore of his native country contains archetypes and images with resemblances to those crafted by Homer and Lycophron. Some theorists speculate that astonishing cultural exchanges are based on rare but actual contacts, usually through commerce. However, I suspect they have causes that are less circumstantial, based on common emotions and universal celebrations.

In his 1919 essay, "Tradition and the Individual Talent," T. S. Eliot asserts: "The existing monuments form an ideal order among themselves, which is modified by the introduction of the new (the really new) work of art among them." He assumes a reciprocal process: Just as art of the past influences the present, the artist of the present transforms the past by assimilation.

Today, more than ever, we find literature a continuum, with every work of art related to every other. In fact, where Eliot wrote of "traditions"—referring, for example, to the Metaphysicals, or the Elizabethans—I would extend his observation to say there are many cultures, but only one tradition. One vast tradition comprises black, white, Asian, woman, man, Christian, Jew,

Muslim, Buddhist. It contains works of conflicting aesthetic persuasions, all "modifying" one another, to use Eliot's term, and all available in our bookstores, concert halls, and galleries.

As I write this now, I am surrounded by cultures, all of them beautiful. Without getting up from my desk I can see, on the shelves around me, a translation of the *Gilgamesh* by David Ferry; an anthology of Chinese poetry edited by Donald Finkel; Lu Chi's *Wen Fu*, a new translation by Sam Hamill; William Matthews's versions of Martial in his *Selected Poems and Translations;* anthologies of Russian poetry and of African poetry; and a program from the Barbican Theatre in London, for Sophocles' Theban trilogy in a new translation by Timberlake Wertenbaker, with choric dances that include, appropriately, African and Asian dances that may have informed ancient drama.

I caught those books at a glance, and I'm sure I omitted many, whose names I may have excluded but whose presence is assured. As I've said, Whitman praised Judaism not by naming it in his poems but by incorporating the rhythms of its liturgy; Henry James honored Jewish immigrants in his prose, not in the content but in the vigorous language. So too, those unnamed books are luminous questions in my mind. The less I am aware of their implications, the larger they grow. However I may wish to, I cannot exclude even those that seem remote from my own life and art. They are alive in me, and they will not be silent.

NOTES

1. Harold Bloom, *Agon: Towards a Theory of Revisionism* (New York: Oxford University Press, 1983), p. 181.

2. Henry James, *The American Scene* (New York: Simon and Schuster, 1906), p. 131.

3. Walt Whitman, *Walt Whitman at the New York Aurora, Editor at 22: A Collection of Recently Discovered Writings,* edited by Joseph Jay Rubin and Charles H. Brown (State College, PA: Bald Eagle Press, 1950). All citations here are to pp. 31–33.

4. Walt Whitman, *Rivulets of Prose: Critical Essays,* edited by Carolyn Wells and Alfred Goldsmith (Freeport, NY: Books for Libraries Press, 1969), pp. 47–48.

5. Justin Kaplan, *Walt Whitman: A Life* (New York: Simon and Schuster, 1980), p. 70.

6. Willard Trask, "King Denis of Portugal," in *Translation VI* (Winter 1978–79), pp. 10–11.

All direct citations to Whitman's poetry are to the following: *Walt Whitman's Leaves of Grass: The First (1855) Edition* (New York: Viking Press, 2005); and *Walt Whitman, Leaves of Grass: Comprehensive Reader's Edition*, edited by Harold W. Blodgett and Scully Bradley (New York: Norton, 1965).

Letter to a Young Poet

Dear _____:

Today, when asked for a "letter to a young poet," I hesitated, just as I do of you when you ask for guidance, because I am unconvinced that such counsel is of value. Literature reveals that advisers should be doubted, from Shakespeare's Polonius, "Neither a borrower or a lender be," to Ezra Pound's Mr. Nixon, who tells Hugh Selwyn Mauberley, "And give up verse, my boy, / There's nothing in it." I've always believed in Sartre's conviction that our decisions are self-generated, whether or not they echo our counselors. At the very least, we are responsible for them.

Even at its best, advice can ring hollow. It is all an artist can do to convey the truth of a moment in time, or just how one is changed profoundly by watching a light-spangled leaf, let alone the right course for another's life or work.

Now Rilke's "Letters to a Young Poet," the basis for the request, does represent advice at its best. Rilke's directives to Franz Xaver Kappus contain truths that are, in a word, indispensable: "Seek the depth of things," he tells his correspondent, and "The necessary thing is after all but this: solitude, great inner solitude." Most important, when he writes of knowing the world in its fullness, Rilke amplifies the poet's call to praise. Still, those maxims outgrow their form. That is, while Rilke's epistolary observations are informative, they are far more sublimely moving when they appear in his poems. For example, here is the same idea of praise as he presents it

Originally appeared in *Teachers & Writers*, vol. 33, no. 1 (Sept.–Oct. 2001).

so powerfully transformed, some twenty years later, in the great *Sonnets to Orpheus,* these lines from Stephen Mitchell's translation:

> Praising is what matters! He was summoned for that,
> and came to us like the ore from a stone's silence.

We who write are forever learners, even when we presume to instruct. I surmise that Rilke was less interested in elucidating Kappus than he was in defining for himself, in a prose narrative, themes that persisted in his poetry. Like Rilke, Theodore Roethke was a generous adviser, voicing aphorisms such as "It is well to keep in touch with chaos," collected in *Straw for the Fire.* Reading his great poem, "The Far Field," an account of a journey to the inner self, I gather that those notebook jottings actually are admonitions to himself as a writer, words that bind together the images and ideas in his poems.

As for the term "young poet," it makes no more sense than any other group designation. A poet who continues to be a poet remains young in essential ways. Wise though they are, Rilke's letters to Kappus, written when Rilke himself was a young poet, are more crotchety than the generous correspondence of his later years.

In literary friendships, age is seldom a factor: while age may divide one writer's work from another in theme or tone, fundamental aesthetic values are binding. When I was still in my teens, I grew close to a family friend some forty years my senior. In succeeding years, she made it clear that our friendship could grow only if I addressed her as a colleague. Often she would ask for my sense of a particular line or image in her latest poem. Once she discouraged my callow adulation, wanting me to see her only as she was, and in her reluctance I knew that if I gave her a gilded mask, I would lose the face beneath. After an inward struggle I accepted her terms, and our conversations deepened. In that reciprocal bond I gained from her insights, she from mine.

And you, my friend, who set your store by transforming what moves you into lines that move others, have as much to teach me as I you. You remind me of my own spontaneity, a quality my contemporaries may have but hold in check. I see in you my own joy in reading aloud a draft I've just printed out, and how anything—a conversation, a chance meeting, a gallery visit, a glimpse of new tulips—can bring about a revelation. It happens to me still, and I wish always to remember that it is I, not the event, who have caused the change. And if you should tell me that friends regardless of age share those experiences, I would answer: Of course. The years between do not matter.

And so, my dear _____, I cannot write that letter any more than I can provide the keys you ask of me. And perhaps, if you disabuse yourself of the expectation, you will find yourself without a mentor. Alone. Only then can you fall to the bottom of Rilke's rock from which altars are built.

Yours,

Octavio Paz

Man of Two Worlds

"Poetry is the secret religion of the modern age," said Octavio Paz (1914–98), who won the Nobel Prize for his great achievement in 1990. He was at once a solitary poet and man of the contemporary world, seeking always to unify the two. A Mexican national, he was well known in the United States for such works as *The Labyrinth of Solitude* and *Sor Juana, or the Traps of Faith.*[1]

The basis for his duality can be found in two books composed in the 1960s and translated into English in 1973. Both books contain his essential poetics, and bear the impact of his residence in India, where he had served for six years as ambassador from Mexico. Although Paz began writing *Alternating Current* (*Corriente alterna*) in 1958, it did not appear in Mexico until 1964; and although the first edition of *The Bow and the Lyre* (*El arco y la lira*) was published in 1956, it is the second edition, of 1967, on which the English version is based.[2]

During their composition, Ambassador Paz, living in Delhi, was profoundly affected by Eastern thought, especially the Buddhist current of Nagarjuna and his commentators. That he was equally engaged with world events is evident from his resignation in 1968, after the democratic movement in Mexico, led by the students, was abruptly ended with the massacre of several hundred peaceful demonstrators. In Delhi on October 3, a few months after a slaughter that took place during the Olympics, Paz wrote "Mexico: 1968 Olympiad." In that poem, he makes real horror more terrifying by presenting it in dreamlike images.

A new version, revised and updated, of an essay that appeared in *The Hudson Review,* vol. 27, no. 3 (Autumn 1974).

La verguenza es ira
Vuelta contra uno mismo:
           Si
Una nacion enter a se averguenza
Es león que se agazapa
Para saltar.
           (Los empleados
Municipales lavan la sangre
En la Plaza de los Sacrificios.)

           Shame is anger
Turned against oneself:
           If
An entire nation is shamed
It is a lion crouched
To spring.
           (Municipal employees
Are washing blood away
In the Plaza de los Sacrificios.)[3]

Octavio Paz is a living incarnation of those tensions in modern poetry between human commitment and aesthetic concern, a dialectic that is fundamental to the art of all nations. And his poetics places the poet at the heart of modern life, singing his solitary song in company with the massed voices of human solitude. In his view, the poet does not speak the language of society but turns away from it, gaining strength in exile.

From the early twentieth century onward, poets pressed to a keen awareness of human misery have worked toward an austere art. At an extreme, poets who have been acutely conscious of modern horror have subordinated the music of poetry to argument and sacrificed the personal vision that informs their art. Since around 1925, a reaction against individuality, as well as against rhetorical devices, has grown more severe with each generation. Often it appears as if the greater an artist's revulsion from destruction, the stronger is his reluctance to indulge his personal perceptions.

In fact, the Renaissance concept of the individual has dwindled in that modern poetry of which Hopkins, Whitman, and Baudelaire were progenitors. The lack of inner wholeness as he perceived it led the Portuguese poet Fernando Pessoa (1888–1935) to write in four voices, naming each one individually (his own name means person). And after around 1945, consciousness of brutality became so acute, especially in European writers, that poetry of the person, however divided, was considered an impossible indulgence. The poet who reported the world in crisis wrote of inner fragmentation as well as outward disaster, and often retreated into silence under the pressure of that disruption.

Paz, too, was acquainted with suffering. He was undivided, though, given a vision of personal integrity. He maintained that the artist, rebuffed by a community that would substitute technological priorities for spiritual growth, transcended those social limitations and ransomed his dying world. What is more, Paz believed that political crisis nourishes great literature, although the people may not be aware of a poet's genius at the time he is writing. And that is natural, for poetry, with its plurality of meanings, seldom is read for what the words convey: the works of St. John of the Cross, for example, were read originally for their exemplary value, rather than for their beauty.

In the work of Octavio Paz, poetry lives on the deepest levels of being, while ideology constitutes superficial layers of consciousness. That is so even in times of crisis. His faith in the power of language to reveal truth makes him affirm that poetry renews daily life and creates meaning in the present. Just as Confucius was said to have called for the reform of language when asked what he would do to administer his country, Paz affirms that the poet who is committed to his art rebuilds empires.

In his books, unending emphasis is laid on the poet's power to resuscitate a lifeless world. Here the poet discovers a sacred knowledge by confronting his deepest feelings in the practice of his art. In that encounter, he perceives unity in a universe that had appeared fragmented: "*el día y la noche reconciliado fluyen como un río manso*" ("the day and the night flow in reconciliation like a gentle river"). By seizing the truth revealed to him in the present moment, he knows that all faces are one face and centuries are confined to an instant: "*no hay nada frente a mi, sólo un instante / rescatado esta noche*" ("there is nothing in front of me, only an instant / recovered tonight").

That sense of unity is the result of a dramatic change in his poetics that took place three decades ago. In an essay entitled

"Poetry and the Reader," Ruth Needleman writes that in the 1930s and 1940s, Paz had stressed the importance of drawing the reader into a creative relationship with the poem but that after that, he shifted his attention to the work of art as a self-sufficient reality.[4]

Earlier in his life, the Mexican poet had been attracted to the collective experiments of the French surrealists, and inspired by Lautréamont's prediction that eventually poetry would be written by everyone. In the 1960s, though, Paz placed his faith in the poet's inventive genius, rather than on the size of his audience.

Between the collectivist leanings of his youth and the spiritual vision of his later years, the poet's life followed a dialectic pattern that is, curiously, analogous to the lives or poetic roles of other Western writers. At an extreme, Baudelaire wavered between aristocratic and revolutionary positions, while Rilke shifted continually between the personae of nobleman and outcast. In the case of Octavio Paz, various political and literary influences molded his thought: Siding with the Republicans in civil war Spain, he felt revolutionary in spirit but came to distrust revolutionary theories. After a short stay in Paris, Paz returned to Mexico in 1938, where he wrote about international politics for *El Popular,* a union newspaper. Then, breaking with the communists, he withdrew from political activity at the time of the Munich pact. During World War II, Paz met Leonora Carrington and other surrealist artists who found refuge in Mexico. And after the war, he met André Breton and Benjamin Péret in Paris and discovered in his own response to surrealism a liberating vitality that recalled his attractions to Blake, Novalis, and Hölderlin. According to the tenets of surrealism, the poet's imagination, cleansed in the fire of the creative act, had the sacred power to rescue the contemporary world.

For all his divagation, these works of the 1950s and 1960s read like the testimony of a man who has witnessed the destruction of all images and then found in the resurrection of those images a creative, sustaining force. In *Alternating Current,* a collection of short essays, and in *The Bow and the Lyre,* a treatise on aesthetics, Paz describes a poetic universe that transcends a world he knows well. Vacillating between patriotism and rebellion, political activity and artistic solitude, Paz found in pure art the preserving strength of our world. It was as though he had found stars at the bottom of hell.

If Paz envisions an art that goes beyond contraries, he allows that it normally moves between two poles which he calls the magical and the revolutionary. In *The Bow and the Lyre*, he says that the magical extreme consists of a desire to return to the natural world, "to sink forever into animal innocence or to free oneself from the weight of history." The revolutionary endeavor, on the other hand, requires a recovery of the alienated consciousness. And although his poetry is alive with a constant dialectical tension between the magical and the revolutionary aims, the impulse that commands his art is the drive to surpass those poles.

The poetics of Octavio Paz is built on his belief in pure time, to which the poet has access. Where calendar time, the rhythm that governs daily life, attaches an end to days and years, mythical time creates life: "The mythical date arrives if a series of circumstances combine to reproduce the event," Paz writes in *The Bow and the Lyre*, and tells of one of the ancient rites of fire, in which the Valley of Mexico, submerged in shadow, suddenly glows in firelight from the Hill of the Star. The poetry of Paz incarnates this view of time. In *"Vida Entrevista"* ("Glimpse of Life"), an early poem, he cries: *"Oh mundo, todo es noche / y la vida es relampago"* ("Oh world, all is night, / life is a lightning-flash"). In a later poem, *Piedra de Sol* (*Sun Stone*), the poet as believer, dejected by year's end, seeking a still point in the present, wanders through the city to find a vision of time's incarnation.

By the process of rhythmic repetition, the poem invokes the myth that returns to begin a new cycle. Octavio Paz believes that language, like the universe, is generated by rhythms that manage separation and union, harmony and discord. That double rhythm is the scaffolding of most cultures, he says: just as the ancient Chinese saw the universe as the cyclical combination of Yin and Yang that form the Tao, the Greeks conceived the cosmos as a struggle and fusion of opposites. And his conjecture recalls that modern poetry is heir to William Blake's union of antinomies in *The Marriage of Heaven and Hell*, as well as to the truth of his assertion: "Without Contraries is no progression."

Although he had embraced contraries from the beginning of

his writing career, Paz in India found in Tantric thought and in Hindu religious life dualities enforcing his conviction that history turns on reciprocal rhythms. In *Alternating Current,* he writes that the Hindu gods, creators or destroyers according to their name and region, manifest contradiction. "Duality," he says, "a basic feature of Tantrism, permeates all of Hindu religious life: male and female, pure and impure, left and right. . . . In Eastern thought, these opposites can co-exist; in Western philosophy, they disappear for the worst reasons: far from being resolved into a higher synthesis, they cancel each other out, due to a gradual deterioration of values."

In fact, the title, *Alternating Current,* refers to those opposites the poet contains either in joy or in anguish: language and silence, solitude and communion, fall and resurrection. The image, of an electric flow that reverses its direction at regular intervals, suggests the galvanic excitement that oscillating rhythms can generate in art.

"Another art is dawning," Paz declares, and predicts that poetry's departure from the linear time of modern progress will be even more radical than the change that two centuries ago altered the Christian notion of a motionless eternity. The art he foresees will be based on a concept of time that recurs, as in ritual, and on a present that incorporates the past and future. Paz writes that the new poetry was inaugurated by Apollinaire, who juxtaposed different spaces within a single poem, and by Eliot and Pound, who used texts from other times and languages in their works. Paz calls the rising poetry an "art of conjugation"; he sees the artist as one who exists in a state of blessed confusion, for he holds in his mind other eras, languages, and continents.

Paz assumes that the modern "ritual" of hallucinogenic drugs, especially widespread in the 1960s, implies a severe criticism of our world's linear time. When people use drugs, he speculates, they perceive the wholeness of life and death, the unity of men and women. Their sensibilities altered, they see the absence of frontiers between people and nations. But Paz feels that the drug experience—like meditation, fasting, and ascetic discipline—is a false road to the spiritual oneness that poetry provides. He maintains that the total surrender required by Buddhism and Tantrism is only analogous to the dedication poetry demands. For the poet actually creates new life, making the day begin again and compressing all time into an instant, knowing

> *lo que pasó no fue pero está siendo*
> *y silenciosamente desemboca*
> *en otro instante que se desvanece*

> what has happened is not past but now exists
> and silently flows
> into another instant that vanishes

—Sun Stone

The structure of *Alternating Current* supports its argument that completeness depends upon the rhythmic assertion of contradictory realities. The essays of its framework—prose poems, really—shine like revelations. His blazing prose, though, dwindles in the English translation, and the periodic structure, however integrated with the theme, is not the clearest setting for his luminous ideas.

The Bow and the Lyre, on the other hand, his most comprehensive discourse on poetic theory, is a book to be grateful for. He speaks as a passionate explorer, recalling his remark that the verb *querer,* which means to desire, comes from the Latin *quaerere* and connotes inquiry. Paz wrote that Breton, his friend and mentor during the years in Paris, combined passion with inquiry in his quest for the word. Besides describing all poetic activity, the word *querer* seems to characterize the poetics of Paz, which is at once a program for poetry and a vital quest for the truth about such disparate things as language, erotic love, and political freedom.

In that book, Paz writes that rhythm and imagery reveal the world's unity. While rhythm is an alternating current that moves language and the universe, imagery, which also oscillates between contraries, reconciles disparate meanings without suppressing any. (St. John's "silent music" combines antithetical things as does the tragic heroine, Antigone, who is torn between divine piety and human law.) Like rhythm, imagery comes from primordial time: if rhythm generates new cycles, imagery closes the gap between name and object that was unknown to primitive man.

Because of the unity they provide, poets have access to a primordial sensibility in which opposites are one, a state reminiscent of Freud's description of the unconscious as a place where antithetical things appear to be the same. This state, though fundamental to art, horrifies Western man. The truth we learn from Paz is that in magical moments—when we see light strike water or watch rock-hollows suck sea—we know that life and death are a totality, not a dilemma.

Paz commits himself to the integrity of all things, and that dedication fires his enthusiasm for surrealism and Buddhism. The same energy generates his study of 1967 emphasizing structuralism in art. In *Claude Lévi-Strauss o el nuevo festín de sopo* (published here as *Claude Lévi-Strauss: An Introduction*)[5] he asserts that so-called primitive men were actually rational because they saw man and time flow through one another.

Nor does his view allow languages to be separable. All languages, in his philosophy, have in common that split between words and the things they signify. If language itself is a translation, then the gap between languages is far less compelling than the distance between names and objects.

The solidarity he proposes supports his great plan to communicate with everyone, regardless of language or culture. "I believe that Western poetry is one," he told Anthony Rudolf in an interview that appeared in *Modern Poetry in Translation* (vol. 11, no. 5). "I believe profoundly in its unity. At the same time I believe in its plurality." The paradox typifies those Buddhist tenets that informed his thought in the 1960s: poetry, like beauty and life, is whole and yet contains many discordant things. It is idle to simplify its complexity or to deny its totality.

The poems of Octavio Paz have attracted various American translators, including Mark Strand, Elizabeth Bishop, and Muriel Rukeyser. *The Collected Poems, 1957–1987,* translated by Eliot Weinberger, includes selections from thirteen books, three of them comprising long poems. The poems divide almost neatly into the major phases of the poet's activity, the early volumes covering the period of surrealist influence; the later, beginning with *Configurations,* enclosing the innovative work of the late 1950s and 1960s. In *Configurations,* a name signifying the form produced by the relative disposition of parts, meanings emerge from explosive phrases that correspond to a universe that we see in an alternating current, as a whole and as bits of a whole. As novel as this may sound, however, the power of his art lies in his vibrant marriage of opposites—sound and silence, attraction and repulsion—in methods as traditional as Blake's fusion of heaven and hell, or Dante's union of light and dark. And although Paz's images of opposition may flow from the alternating rhythms of separation and union he found in the cultures of the world, they suggest very strongly the antinomies found in all great poetry. But then, the most original poetry always tends to draw its newness from conventional means.

The poetry of Octavio Paz is at once of Mexico and of the world, moving beyond nations to reach the inner lives of people everywhere. That universality is what the surrealists hoped to achieve when they diminished the role of author and called for the intervention of the unconscious in poetic creation. Paz is a characteristic Mexican. He draws on a rich Aztec heritage and on his American Indian ancestry. If his mind is disciplined by European poetic forms, he envisions the vast empty areas of space that are central to poets born in the Americas. He is one of several Latin-American diplomat-poets: not only Darío and Neruda, but also Mexican poet-ambassadors affected him. His countrymen were José Gorostiza, from whom he absorbed techniques for the long poem, and José Juan Tablada, who attracted Paz for the way he fused European forms and haiku to liberate the structures of his poetry.

If the background of his poetry is Mexican, its impulse is to reach outward toward all people. "The poet is the reader of the book of the universe," Paz remarked in an interview with Rita Guibert, referring to a Renaissance metaphor used by romantic poets. "Aesthetic styles and trends transcend nationality and have nothing to do with frontiers. . . . Modern literature is *one*, despite the plurality of languages and traditions. . . . Styles are historic, they have never been exclusively national, and they leap across walls and frontiers. . . . A writer is always a plurality of voices, every language is a plurality of languages."[6]

Paz recited those beliefs when he spoke of his *Renga*, a work named for a Japanese collective poetic form. *Renga* is a sonnet sequence composed in 1969 in four languages by Paz; Charles Tomlinson, an Englishman; Eduardo Sanguineti, an Italian; and Jacques Roubaud, a Frenchman. It is emblematic of his poetry: just as he merged his deepest thoughts with those of foreign poets, his voice is the confluence of many voices.

In the "Prologue" to the early collection, that voice is heard: "Against silence and noise I invent the Word, freedom that invents itself and invents me every day." Like Whitman, Paz uses the self as metaphor to permit discoveries on a deep psychic level, and to merge with others. Just as Whitman creates in *Leaves of Grass* an observer who identifies with every leaf, star, and atom, Paz constructs a speaker who sees nature as an organic part of the soul: "I go forward slowly and I people the night with stars, with speech, with the breathing of distant water waiting for me where the dawn appears."

Paz envisions a place that is unfragmented by time, undivided by "what I have been" or "what I will become." This discovery is prominent in Paz's *Early Poems, 1935–1955*, translated by Muriel Rukeyser and others. Take, for example, the following poems excluded from Weinberger's 669-page English edition, *Collected Poems, 1957–1987*.[7] First, "*Más allá del amor*" ("Beyond Love") shows that place

> Beyond ourselves,
> On the frontier of being and becoming,
> a life more alive claims us

In contrast, he portrays the modern world as territory where existence is limited by the deadly notion of rectilinear time. Only in radiant moments can wholeness be found. In another early exclusion from the 1987 English edition of *Collected Poems,* "*Semillas para un himno*" ("Seeds for a Psalm"), the poet sees islands "in flames in mid-Pacific" and "the polar night on fire" and knows that love has appeared in an unworthy country, a "land condemned to repeat itself without respite."

Early on, the poet is seen as a visionary who focuses his igneous gaze on the world and sees life as alive. De Sade, in "*El prisoniero*" ("The Prisoner"), is addressed in this way:

Comet whose body is substance, whose tail glitters in
    dialectics,
You rush through the nineteenth century holding a grenade
    of truth,
exploding as you come to our own time.

Especially in his early work, poetry is an alchemy whose agents of transmutation are fire and water. In "*Lección de cosas*" ("Object Lesson"), those images have a hypnotic, ritual pull: "Facing water, days of fire. / Facing fire, days of water." As for "*El cantáro roto*" ("The Broken Waterjar"), the poet as open-eyed spectator sees the stars as "bracelets of flaming islands" and knows that "life and death are not opposite worlds, we are one stem with twin flowers." In an enraptured moment the surrealists would have coveted, he finds the universe uncut and no part of the self suppressed.

In fact, the dominating image of his poetry, early and late, is the mystic oxymoron of burned water. The phrase is glossed in a note to a later poem, "Return," which made its debut in *The Hudson Review* in spring 1972. The note, though subsequently altered, first appeared in this way:

> *Atl tlachinolli:* burned water—not burning water, as it has
> been sometimes translated—water in flames, as the "wet
> flame" of Novalis. The Aztecs, in their   wanderings around
> the lake of Mexico (today an urban desert of saltpeter) saw
> a bundle floating in the waters. They fished it out and
> found two wood sticks for making fire. The meaning
> was *atl tlachinoli:* the marriage of fire and water. This
> metaphor was the founding stone of Mexico-Tenochtitlan.

In that poem, the speaker returns to a city to find "thoroughfares of scars / alleys of living flesh." There

The signs were broken

                    atl tlachinolli

                                            was split

                    burnt water

There is no center

                    plaza of congregation and
                        consecration

there is no axis

                    the years dispersed

To depict the fallen city, the poet distorts syntax in an approximation of the rotting bond between government and people. The device recalls Dante's breakdown of language to indicate the disruption of social order. In the *Inferno,* which incarnates a vision of godlessness and political discordance, Dante hears Pluto utter *"Pape Satàn, Pape Satàn, aleppe,"* and hears the souls of the Sullen, buried in mire, gurgling a grotesque parody of a hymn.

In these poems, water is transfigured by its relation to fire, as conflicts are resolved in visions of unity. In "Mutra," another of the early poems excluded from the 1987 English edition, *Collected Poems,* the poet sees "water of stars and reptiles, forests of burnt water and bodies" and declares "no quiero ser / Dios, no quiero ser a tientas, no quero regresar, soy hombre y el homre es / el hombre . . ." "I do not want to be / God, I do not want to grope in the dark, I am / a man . . ." Although the experience is precisely godlike, since the poet has reached a transcendence of contraries, Paz uses it to epitomize manhood.

In the later poems, Paz finds his divided world redeemed. The central figure of "Salamander," a transitional poem of the late 1950s, is an animal and a sacred presence, as well as the mythical creature that can endure fire without harm. The poet sees it as having ambivalent qualities:

> Salamandra
> nombre antiguo del fuego
> > (y antídotao antiguo
> > contra el fuego)
>
> Salamander
> ancient name of fire
> > (and ancient
> > antidote to fire)[8]

Beholding the changing amphibian, the poet knows that life "does not commence without blood / Without the embers of sacrifice." The poem rises in a marvelous ritual chant for life and destruction; just as fire nourishes and destroys, the passion of one feeds and kills the other:

Hablas como una fuente

Salamandra
                    espiga
hija del fuego
espíritu del fuego
condensación de la sangre
sublimación de la sangre
evaporación de la sangre

Salamandra de aire
la roca es llama
                    la llama es humo

you speak
                    as a fountain speaks
Salamander
                    blade of wheat
daughter of fire
spirit of fire
condensation of blood
sublimation of blood
evaporation of blood

Salamander of air
the rock is flame
                    the flame is smoke

That blend is a major instance of Paz's reading of the world as a collection of fragments that become more themselves in relation to other things. As his title, *Configurations,* indicates, objects assume their real identity in the structure of the whole: fire becomes fire in its opposition to water; man becomes more himself in his interconnection with another being. In "Signs in Rotation," a section he added in 1965 to *The Bow and the Lyre,* Paz defines the poem as a "vibrant space on which a few signs are projected like an ideogram," and as "fragments that regroup and seek to form a figure, a nucleus of meanings." He asserts that the world has been split apart:

In antiquity the universe had one form and one center; its movement was; governed by a cyclical rhythm . . . The political order and the order of the poem, public festivals and private rites—and even discord and the transgressions of the universal rule—were manifestations of the cosmic rhythm. Later, the figure of the world widened: space became infinite or transfinite; the Platonic year turned into a linear, unending succession; and stars ceased to be the image of cosmic harmony. The center of the world was displaced and God, ideas, and essences disappeared. We were alone.

Because the universe is no longer complete, "space expands and breaks apart," time is disrupted and the self is dissolved. But Paz views that dissolution as a strengthening power, for it causes each fragment to be dependent on other parts.

That sense of otherness is central to *Sun Stone,* Paz's great transitional poem named for the Aztec calendar wheel whose elements, sun and stone, incarnate the unity of life and death. The speaker, the poet on a quest, seeks a day that is alive, a year that does not end in death. In an erotic union, he sees the natural and supernatural worlds combined:

> I am the other when I am myself, my acts
> are more my own when they are everybody's
> because to be myself I must be other,
> go out of myself, seek myself among others,
> those others who are not if I do not exist

To be himself, he calls forth an otherness that has not been allowed to exist: "The world changes," he cries, "if two look at each other and see, / to love is to undress our names."

With renewed vision, he sees that the cry of the victim and the cry of the hangman are one:

son llamas

> *os ojos y son llamas lo que miran,*
> *lama la oregja y el sonido llama,*
> *brasa los labios y tízón la lengua,*
> *el tacto y lo que toca, el pensamiento*
> *y lo pensado, llama el que lo piensa*

> they are flames
> the eyes are flames and those who gaze are flaming
> the ear is fire and the fiery music,
> live coal the lips and the tongue firebrand,
> the one who touches and the one who is touching,
> thinker and thought, and the thinker is a fire

Like an ancient fire ritual, *Sun Stone* invokes the myth that reforms the present moment, bringing new energy to earthly things. The land reborn, the poem returns to its beginnings, with identical lines about a river that "advances and retreats, goes roundabout, / arriving for ever."

Paz's work of the 1960s, *Blanco* (1966) and some of the poems in *Ladera Este* (1968), embodies his belief that as art moves closer to ritual the artist, who creates in exile, is drawing society to him. "The Balcony" is one of the poems in which Delhi is used as an image of the modern world. The speaker leans out on a balcony, precariously "nailed / in the middle of the whirlwind" perceiving "this distance that is so near / I do not know what to name it." Feeling close to a city that lies like "a violated corpse," he sees that life and death vanish "in the same flashing sea'" and knows, in an incandescent moment,

> *sobre este frágil puente de palabras*
> *La hora me levana*
> *hambre de encarnación padece el tiempo*
> *Más allá de mí mismo*
> *en algún lado aguardo mi llegada*
>
> Over this fragile bridge of words
> The hour lifts me up
> Time suffers from a hunger for incarnation
> Somewhere beyond myself
> I await my arrival[9]

Blanco, one of his most ambitious poems, was composed in Delhi during the summer of 1966. It bodies forth a meeting between East and West, language and silence, the self and the other. Those opposites are presented as dialogue that propels the poem forward, leading to an instant of coherence:

                    You are naked
          As a syllable
                         As a flame
          An island of flames
          Passion of compassionate coals
          The world
                    a bundle of your images
          Drowned in music
                         Your body
          Flowing through my body
                                   Seen
          Vanished
                    It makes real the seeing

   The poetry of Octavio Paz is an urgent matter because it in-
sists on the wholeness of life, love, and nations, a unity that only
art can reveal. And if I have always known that poetry lives on
the deepest levels of the world's being, the voice of Octavio Paz
commands me to admit the rightness of this knowledge. For Paz
sees the world burning, and knows with visionary clarity that opposites are resolved in a place beyond contraries, in a moment
of pure vision: in that place, there are no frontiers between men
and women, life and death. If his poetry incarnates the mind's
journey toward insight, his voyage is my voyage, his passion my
passion:

          tonight is my life, and this single moment
          which never stops opening, never stops revealing
          where my life lay, who I was, what your name is
          and what my own name is
                                            —*Sun Stone*

   The truth I see darkly in the poetry of Octavio Paz is the basic
fact of lost unity and "how vulnerable it is / to be women and
men, the glory it is to be man"

     y compartir el pan, el sol, la muerte
     el olvidado asombro de estar vivos;
     amar es combatir, si dos se besan
     el mundo cambia, encarnan los deseos,

and share our bread and share our sun and our death,
the dark forgotten marvel of being alive;
to love is to struggle, and if two people kiss
the world is transformed

—Sun Stone

In a world that has more false shamans than true poets, the poetry of Octavio Paz is real, for he has created an image of man going beyond himself. The bow represents man's ability to shoot himself beyond his condition, and the lyre figures forth the place in the cosmos for human endeavor. Although Paz frequently makes original use of imagery from Buddhism and Aztec lore, his true concern is poetry's godlike power. And he makes me say: Of course. I have always known it was so. I believe it also.

NOTES

1. *El laberinto de la soledad* (1950), English translation by Lysander Kemp (Grove Press, 1961). *Sor Juana Inés de la Cruz; o, Las trampas de la fe* (1982). English translation by Margaret Sayers Peden (Harvard University Press, 1982).

2. *Alternating Current*, by Octavio Paz, translated by Helen R. Lane (Viking); *The Bow and the Lyre*, by Octavio Paz, translated by Ruth L. C. Simm (University of Texas Press).

3. Translation mine. Unless otherwise specified, I've kept my translations, which appeared in the original version of this piece. Newer translations appear in *Collected Poems, 1957–1987*, edited and translated into English by Eliot Weinberger, "with additional translations by Elizabeth Bishop, Paul Blackburn, Lysander Kemp, Denise Levertov, John Frederick Nims, and Charles Tomlinson" (New Directions, 1987).

4. In "Octavio Paz Symposium" of *Books Abroad: An International Literary Quarterly*, vol. 46, no. 4 (Autumn 1972), pp. 550–51.

5. Translated by J. S. Bernstein and Maxine Bernstein (Cornell University Press, 1970).

6. *Seven Voices: Seven Latin American Writers Talk to Rita Guibert*, translated by Frances Partridge (New York, 1973), pp. 208, 209, 231.

7. Excluded poems appear in *Early Poems* by Octavio Paz, translated by Muriel Rukeyser and others (New Directions, 1973). Apart from

Rukeyser, this book includes versions by Paul Blackburn, Lysander Kemp, and William Carlos Williams.

8. The translation of "Salamander" in *The Hudson Review* first drew me to the genius of Octavio Paz.

9. Translations of "The Balcony" and *Sun Stone* are by Muriel Rukeyser.

Paul Celan
Poet of Silence

Paul Celan, the great midcentury poet who found resonance in the silence of loss, belongs to at least three cultural traditions. He wrote in German, influenced primarily by Rilke, Friedrich Hölderlin and Georg Trakl. He was a Jew, a survivor of the Holocaust who wrote devastating poetry about the Nazi horror without ever naming it. He spoke perfect French, admired Rimbaud, and spent his mature years in Paris, where he died a suicide in 1970 at the age of 49.

He was born Paul Antschel in the city of Czernowitz in Bukovina, a part of Northern Romania that he called "a region inhabited by people and books." It was a section where Jews had enjoyed relative freedom from the late 18th century until 1941, when the Nazi slaughters began. In June 1942, when the Nazis began deporting citizens to labor camps in the Transnistria district of the Ukraine, where most of them died, Celan implored his parents to follow him into hiding. They resisted, and he fled alone, only to return and find them gone. One year later, sent himself to a forced labor camp in Romania, he learned they had been murdered. He escaped or was released in 1944. Like Primo Levi, Celan harbored a sorrow that pursued him to suicide.

In his poetry, Celan used archaisms and neologisms, as well as an interior syntax, in service of a fresh vision. He wanted a new German, partly to convey the horror of his torn world and partly because his mother tongue was the "death-bringing speech" of

---

This essay is new and hitherto unpublished. However, the germ of it may be found in a review I wrote that appeared in *The New York Times Book Review*, p. 22.

the mass exterminator. He referred to the corrosion of existing language as the "horrible falling silent." That silence, born of misery, is the source of his greatness.

His famous poem, "Todesfuge" ("Death Fugue"), is a masterpiece of evocation. It has no punctuation, for there can be no stop, no resting place for the speaker. Famously it begins:

> Black milk of daybreak we drink it at sundown
> we drink it at noon in the morning we drink it at night
> we drink and we drink it
> (Translations by Michael Hamburger)

"Black milk" arrests us, an ultimate paradox. In lines that follow, Celan invents metaphors that have roots in the reality of horror. He writes of graves prisoners are forced to shovel, graves in the ground, graves in air. He portrays a man "in the house," presumably a commandant, who orders prisoners to "play up for the dance," to "sing up and play." Those brief phrases, severe and mysterious, evoke a terrible truth: as we know musicians were ordered to play for grave-digging and executions. He does not tell us that in so many words. Not Celan.

In "Todesfuge," it is the silence that moves us: The last lines are

> your golden hair Margarete
> your ashen hair Shulamith

The first of those lines comes from a letter the boss is writing to his love in Germany. The second ironically echoes the Song of Songs. Their diction and music suggest the ideal Romantic vision, which is harshly undercut by the grave-digging scene.

With an economy of language and daring metaphors, Celan tells of brutality with a transcendence that is genuine. It is made so by his luminous faith and the force of his stubborn praise, and the impact of his blazing light imagery—fires, suns, "bright stones . . . the light bringers," "the light and the Light, lamplike brightness / inside me, just at the point / where most painfully one says, never."

In other hands, under the circumstances celebration of life

would be hard to accept. Celan's austere praise is inevitable, and that is his greatness. Despite his life's darkness, light shines everywhere. It gleams in his images of doves, ice, snow, frost, stars. It dazzles in the ineradicable "tree-high thought" that "tunes in to light's pitch":

> there are
> still songs to be sung on the other side
> of mankind.

Song of Our Cells

There is an eerie resemblance between two books on my shelf that would seem to be worlds apart. They look alike, and have similar titles that are printed in swirling letters on pale-colored jackets: *The Lives of a Cell: Notes of a Biology Watcher*, by Lewis Thomas, and *The Life of Poetry*, by Muriel Rukeyser. Gazing at them, I feared they might have suffered a change that was magical, like alchemy, or natural, like cell fusion—that phenomenon in which two complete, alien genomes become part of a single cell. I separated them, suspecting the books were living things. To begin with, their texts have affinities, as in the following passages:

> We do not have solitary beings. Every creature is, in some sense, connected to and dependent on the rest. . . . There is a tendency for living things to join up, establish linkages, live inside each other, return to earlier arrangements, get along, whenever possible. This is the way of the world.
> —*The Lives of a Cell*

> But our age, in the promise of its science and its poetry, has made available to all people the idea of one world. . . . Contained in this truth is the unity of the imagination.
> —*The Life of Poetry*

In many ways, the two writers could not be less alike. Thomas, a microbiologist and former Dean of Yale Medical School, writes in a seemingly casual but intense, whimsical prose about the nature of living things; Rukeyser, a poet who envisions the

---

This essay first appeared in *The Hudson Review*, vol. 29, no. 1 (Spring 1976).

unity of all people, writes in a vatic tone of poetry's urgency. Despite their differences, though, the charming scientist and the pythonic poet echo one another, communicating, to paraphrase one of Thomas's examples of whale talk, in signals. "Lewis Thomas here," one writer says; "Muriel Rukeyser here," the other answers. Indeed, communication is one of the subjects of their dialogue. "Nature abhors a long silence," Thomas assures us. "The use of truth is its communication," Rukeyser concurs.

In his new book, a collection of essays originally appearing in *The New England Journal of Medicine,* Thomas returns over and again to the theme of unity, finding connectedness to be the principle of living things:

> The new phenomenon of cell fusion . . . is the most unbio-
> logic of all phenomena, violating the most fundamental
> myth of the last century for it denies the importance of
> specificity, integrity, and separateness in living things. Any
> cell—man, animal, fish, fowl, or insect—given the chance
> and under the right conditions, brought into contact with
> any other cell, however foreign, will fuse with it.

And Muriel Rukeyser, writing of art's consequence in American life, argues that poetry reveals the harmony of apparently conflicting ideas. For her, the principle of continuity rules the elements of a poem, governs human assemblage, and links us with our time. "A poem," she writes, "is not its words or its images, any more than a symphony is its notes or a river its drops of water. Poetry depends on the moving relations within itself. It is an art that lives in time, expressing and evoking the moving relation between the individual consciousness and the world."

Central to both books is the imagery of dance. "We live in a dancing matrix of viruses," Thomas asserts, and Rukeyser compares the artist's juxtapositions to "the river meeting the sea in eternal relationship, in a dance of power, in a dance of love."

They are, of course, devoted to different kinds of unity: Lewis Thomas explores the resemblances of all forms of life, each connected to every other and obeying the same laws; Muriel Rukeyser affirms poetry's unifying power. There are, however, impressive areas of overlap. Dr. Thomas provides striking metaphors for poetry when he writes that we share with nearly all living things the urge to make music. His essay, "The Music of *This* Sphere," wakes the heart, for it is, in fact, a modern psalm in praise of song, celebrating the "joyful noise" of all creatures:

> Somewhere, underlying all the other signals, is a continual music. . . . Gorillas beat their chests for certain kinds of discourse. Animals with loose skeletons rattle them, or, like rattlesnakes, get sounds from externally placed structures. Turtles, alligators, crocodiles, and even snakes make various more or less vocal sounds.

Nor does his explanation for the phenomenon diminish its grandeur. He writes: "The rhythmic sounds might be the recapitulation of something else—an earliest memory, a core for the transformation of inanimate, random matter in chaos into the improbable, ordered dance of living forms."

At times he probes the arts for extended analogies, as when he compares the development of words to the evolution of species, writing that language is alive, a great organism moved by cells that are words which fuse and then mate. On other occasions, he minimizes disciplinary frontiers just as he lessens divisions among beings; and informs on various levels. For example, he writes that our process of transferring verbal information is far less precise than other biologic systems for communication—and with good reason. He compares the manner in which we store information to the way lymphocytes are programmed through the receptors on their surfaces to recognize alien substances in the tissues. Carrying through the analogy with the mind, Thomas writes that unlike memory, which can store diverse words and facts, each of the lymphocytes is programmed to recognize only a single molecule. Our minds are capable of creating ambiguity, on which language depends; lymphocytes, on the other hand, must be precise to avoid devastating consequences.

While the scientist's reasoning leads him to poetry, the poet's principles are drawn from science. Muriel Rukeyser's perception of truth is comparable, she believes, to the scientist's apprehension of facts not as isolated things but as phenomena that interact, feeding or destroying one another. Arguing for a "dynamics of poetry," she writes: "We know that the relationships in poetry are clearer when we think in terms of a dynamic system, whose tendencies toward equilibrium, and even toward entropy, are the same as other systems."

What emerges from my reading of both works is the staggering truth of unity, the conviction that all life is part of the same fabric. Together, the writers have a mysterious, insisting, latent voice murmuring, "ONE WORLD, ONE WORLD," that idea established and confirmed by the evidence of microbiology and the findings of criticism. In fact, their joint vision is so compelling that the words "science" and "poetry" seem too narrowly restrictive for truths they uncover.

Rukeyser emphasizes poetry's resolution of components; Thomas stresses that synchrony is the way of the world. To illustrate those beliefs, both draw on abundant examples from primitive cultures, linguistics, technology, history, anthropology, and astronomy, among other fields. In discussing poetry as prophecy, Muriel Rukeyser remarks that subjugated American Indians of California in 1870 found they were dreaming of victory in patterns, and, losing all hope of victory, sang their dreams. And Lewis Thomas, speaking of how living things tend to join up and establish linkages, compares creatures of myth— the Sphinx, the Ch'i-lin of ancient China, the Centaur—to cells. The mythical animals and the cells are hybrid beings, made up of parts that are entirely familiar; both are mixtures of species. The phenomenon of distinct cells fusing becomes, by his witty analogy, "a Chimera, a Griffon, a Sphinx, a Ganesha, a Peruvian god, a Ch'i-lin, an omen of good fortune, a wish for the world."

At times the two authors seem to be writing one book, as when they speculate that the Western fear of death results from an inadequate understanding of its naturalness. Muriel Rukeyser suggests that Walt Whitman's view of life and death as a continuum came as a reaction to America's denial of death, a disavowal she calls "one of the deepest sources, in our culture, of the corruption of consciousness." And Lewis Thomas writes that the custom of dying in hospital secrecy may breed fear of the unfamiliar. When we think of the life of all life, a new picture may emerge: death is never sudden, for cells descend in sequence, a process that takes hours or days. Besides, death is what we have in concert with everything that lives. He says: "Everything dies, all around, trees, plankton, lichens, mice, whales, flies, mitochondria. . . . Flies do not develop a ward round of diseases that carry them off, one by one. They simply age, and die, like flies."

Although Rukeyser and Thomas have the capacity to entertain various kinds of knowledge, they offer more striking insights in their own spheres. Rukeyser reasons that poetry invites a total response: the poet, capturing the reciprocal reality of diverse phenomena, provides a meeting place for our fragmented impressions.

While she writes persuasively of Dante's art of arrangement and Melville's urge to resolve conflicts, she is most inventive when exploring the lesser-known figures, such as James Gates Percival, "the lost poet of meeting places." Percival, a physician and geologist whose poems combined fields of thought, won attention from his nineteenth-century American contemporaries only for conventional, somewhat hackneyed, verses. More startling, however, are the uncelebrated poems that deal with the transcendent harmony of seemingly discordant data. She quotes *Prometheus,* a poem composed in 1822, which begins with a configuration of objects that confounds the mind—comet, star, insect, atom—then moves suddenly into light:

> Truth stands before him in a full, clear blaze
> An intellectual sunbeam . . .

And although he crosses cultural boundaries to find metaphors, Lewis Thomas writes most impressively of microbiology. Underlying his thesis about unity is his conviction that laws of cooperation govern species. He corrects a common misunderstanding, for example, when he mentions that the natural relationship between human beings and microbes is not destructive. In the rare instances when bacteria are harmful to us—usually by a freakish accident on their part—the effects are worse for them than for us. Contrary to popular belief, microbes are not our adversaries: "Disease usually results from inconclusive negotiations for symbiosis, an overstepping of the line by one side or the other, a biologic misinterpretation of borders."

Nor is humankind superior to other species. Thomas observes that our "human chauvinism" causes us to imagine we are detached from and above the rest of life, but that in fact science has destroyed that illusion. "We are shared, rented, occupied," he declares. "Man could not be man without mitochondria, centrioles, basal bodies," he writes, describing the organelles that live in our cells.

Organelles are probably remnants of primitive viruses and bacteria, but he refers to certain organelles, such as mitochondria, as creatures, because they control their own replication. He questions whether the body and the organelles, which carry out vital metabolic functions, can be described accurately as having a master-slave arrangement. On the contrary, he points out that they live inside us, and we, their true servants, have given them a free ride through evolutionary fires. Moreover, the organelles comprise our very being, providing our identity.

His thoughts about organelles call to my mind the generation of Victorian poets whose faith in the natural order was shaken by the publication of Darwin's *Origin of Species*. If it troubled our literary ancestors to learn that man descended from the apes, it might have shattered them to realize that we *haven't* descended from more primitive forms of life: those ancient beings are as much ourselves as our eyes and our hearts.

Most important, he reminds us that we share identical organelles with all living beings. In fact, our organelles are indistinguishable from those of other creatures, probably because all earthly life derived from a single cell. Impassioned, he utters:

> They feel like strangers, but the thought comes that the
> same creatures, precisely the same, are out there in the cells
> of sea gulls, and whales, and dune grass, and seaweed, and
> hermit crabs, and further inland in the leaves of the beech
> in my backyard, and in the family of skunks beneath the
> back fence, and even in that fly on the window. Through
> them, I am connected; I have close relatives, once removed,
> all over the place.

When writing of a common heritage, he soars and glides in passages like that one, which are reminiscent of *Leaves of Grass:*

The sharphoofed moose of the north, the cat on the housesill,
        the chickadee, the prairie-dog,
the litter of the grunting sow as they tug at her
        teats,
the brood of the turkeyhen, and she with her
        halfspread wings,
I see in them and myself the same old law.

Dr. Thomas recalls Whitman in his inspired enumeration of real things, and in his discovery of self through recognizing the uniformity of diverse beings. The microbiologist, however, extends the basis for connecting the self with other beings by divulging the role of organelles in that relationship. And in that sense, he is a realization of Whitman's prophecy, in the Preface to *Leaves of Grass,* that "there shall be love between the poet and the man of demonstrable science."

The combined wisdom of Muriel Rukeyser and Lewis Thomas provides one more indication that discoveries of truth have remarkable affinities, whether they occur in the arts or in the sciences. In many instances, the same truth has been revealed to various minds centuries apart, and applied to different concepts. Discoveries concerning the harmony of opposites, for example, were applied by William Blake to the nature of life and by physicists to the nature of matter. Blake wrote, "Without Contraries is no Progression. Attraction and Repulsion, Reason and Energy, Love and Hate, are necessary to Human Existence." And on the same subject modern physicists, following the discoveries of Niels Bohr and Lord Rutherford, tell us that positively and negatively charged particles achieve a balance in all atoms and molecules, providing them with their structure.

So it is with two discoveries of the image and its relation to creative thought. Ezra Pound wrote, "An 'Image' is that which presents an intellectual and emotional complex in an instant of time. I use the term 'complex' rather in the technical sense employed by the new psychologists, such as Hart. . . ." For Pound, the image was a dynamic, changing thing, in continuous motion. It was not simply a static description but the presentation—in light that moves, in darkness that comes on, in fruit that falls—of the person who sees or hears or touches the object.

If the concept was fundamental to modern poetry, it mattered to science as well, for Albert Einstein described a like process of thought in discussing his own manner of reasoning. In answer to a psychological survey of mathematicians, he wrote: "The words of the language, as they are written or spoken, do not seem to play any role in my mechanism of thought. The physical entities which seem to serve as elements in thought are certain signs and more or less clear images which can be 'voluntarily' reproduced and combined."

Nor do the poet and the scientist differ in their methods of arriving at truth, despite the assertions of generations of Western educators who have urged dividing the arts from the sciences. The revelations of Blake and of the physicists depend, each in its own way, on an experience of knowledge as well as on an intellectual apprehension of a formula. Each supposes a moving process of realization. Each incorporates a dance of images, a wheel of connected contrasts. The reality of each truth is reciprocal, rather than dependent upon isolated facts.

To be sure, there are some essential differences in their processes of discovery. What the poet perceives as truth, the scientist must demonstrate. Then too, all scientific discoveries are built on a scaffolding of previous discoveries over time. In the example given above, Blake's revelation was oracular and is quoted, in fact, from one of the Prophetic Books, *The Marriage of Heaven and Hell.* In contrast, the discoveries of Bohr and Rutherford were built on Dalton's conclusions about the atomic nature of things. And they led, in turn, to studies by modern physicists concerning even smaller particles in atoms.

Nevertheless, I suspect that many important discoveries in science are based on revelation, even in our age when augury is hardly respectable. Reading *The Double Helix,** by Dr. James Watson, the molecular biologist, I was struck by the revelatory way in which the structure of DNA (deoxyribonucleic acid) was discovered. In that compelling adventure story, Dr. Watson recounts

---

The Double Helix: Being a Personal Account of the Discovery of the Structure of DNA (New York, 1968).

how he and Dr. Francis Crick tried to understand how the genetic code worked and to find a structure for all its properties. Finally, they hit upon that structure as a visual image: a double spring, or "helix." Indeed, they *saw* truth.

Further, all works of science and poetry exist in a fabric of time, a pull on one end exerting a change at the other. For example, modern immunologists have proven the validity and, in fact, interdependency of two nineteenth-century theories on the nature of immunity to microbial disease. Curiously, at the time of their formulation the theories were considered antithetical. Dr. Paul Ehrlich held that the body defends itself against infectious disease by means of the substance it makes called antibody. Dr. Eli Metchnikoff claimed that body resistance is affected by cells that become educated in fighting off microorganisms. Contemporary scientists have altered the theories, in effect, by proving both correct: they have transformed them from issues of debate to operative factors.

Poets, too, speak in a lively dialogue with the near and remote past. In John Berryman's *Homage to Mistress Bradstreet*, America's first poet is the object of Berryman's blazing passion. Just as her wholeness and integrity inspire the modern poet, his celebration of her illuminates certain qualities of her life and work. Although he praises her endurance and laments his own instability, his self-examination brings to light the Puritan poet's tendency to question the permanence of assertions:

> I wist not what to wish, yet sure, thought I
>   If so much excellence abide below
> How excellent is He that dwells on High,
>   Whose power and beauty by his works we know.

That kind of reciprocity is found in the work of Marianne Moore, who said frequently that she wrote out of gratitude to books and people. In 1968 she told me, "You'll be reading the French poets, or Wallace Stevens, and you will be influenced. You will have a touch of it in what you write. And in your emotions." An instance of her interaction with the past is her early poem, "Those Various Scalpels," containing a series of epithets that embody a passionate but futile address to a cool beauty:

                    your hair, the tails of two
        fighting-cocks head to head in stone like sculptured
                    scimitars re-
                peating the curve of your ears in reverse order:
                    your eyes, flowers of ice and snow

In that poem, Moore evokes the similes in *The Song of Solomon*
("Thine eyes are as doves behind thy veil"), but makes it new by
using ironic metaphors that objectify the speaker's passion and
playful rebuke. And poets in our time use features of old models such as the riddle and the night chant just as scientists use aspects of the Mendelian laws, which they do not deny but simply
understand in different ways because of the findings of modern
geneticists.

Apart from resembling poetry in its methods and in the nature
of its findings, science can amplify poetry's intuited truths; like
mythology, science has an organizing power for ordering modern
experience. If art reveals the unity of all things by synchronizing
discordant parts, science supports that unity by enlarging the
prospects. We learn from science that cooperation is the law of
life at all levels, and that all beings get along by cooperating,
accommodating, exchanging.

When he speculates that all beings are united, Dr. Thomas
enlarges Muriel Rukeyser's belief in poetry's insistence on unity.
And both statements provide a dynamic commentary on her
Waterlily Fire, a sequence that intimates the connectedness of all
people:

                                    now
                The bridges bind us in symbol, the sea
                Is a bond, the sky reaches into our bodies.
                We pray: we dive into each other's eyes.

And in Rukeyser's translation of *Sun Stone,* by Octavio Paz,
the speaker finds his own individuality paradoxically by discovering what he shares with the other:

                I am the other when I am myself, my acts
                are more my own when they are everybody's
                because to be myself I must be other

The theme occurs also in *Leaves of Grass:*

> And I know that the hand of God is the
> elderhand of my own,
> And I know that the spirit of God is the
> eldest brother of my own,
> And that all the men ever born are also my
> brothers

What science has given underscores the sacredness of every living thing. That emphasis is of supreme importance to the poet, who transforms natural objects into aspects of himself. In D. H. Lawrence's collection of poems, *Birds, Beasts and Flowers,* each of the creatures he presents is a blessed realization of what man must find in himself. And Muriel Rukeyser, whose poetry would reconstruct our way of seeing the world, writes of modern cruelty paradoxically in a way that forces up her praise of what is human. In "Rational Man," a section of her long poem, *Breaking Open,* she enumerates those miseries and concludes: "Mercy, Lord. On every living life."

If the great poets have searched for unity of being, Lewis Thomas has magnified the idea of self by emphasizing that we live in and on one another. As he explored the self, Whitman *observed* the gradual emergence of unity: "I am of the old and the young . . . of the woman the same as of the man." In our time Lewis Thomas has rediscovered the self as a composition of mitochondria, basal bodies, and centrioles, whose basic tendencies are to join up, whose hybrid nature constitutes hope for a divided world. Most subtle and curious of all: Whitman, who wrote that "seeing, hearing and feeling are miracles," also predicted the artistic relevance of science: "Exact science and its practical movements are no checks on the greatest poet but always his encouragement and support." As though in fulfillment of that prophecy, Dr. Lewis Thomas offers his urgent, if dizzying, truth that we are one with all living beings. Moreover, that only by recognizing what we share with other organisms can we revere all forms of life—including our own.

Marianne Moore

A Way of Seeing

When they are read as a modern poetic sequence, three poems by Marianne Moore reveal a manner of perception, a way of seeing beneath surfaces to what is real. The poems are "The Steeple-Jack," "The Student," and "The Hero." Although their first appearance in print was as a sequence called "Part of a Novel, Part of a Poem, Part of a Play" (*Poetry,* 1932), they never appeared that way again. Published separately in various editions, they are set wide apart in Moore's *Complete Poems* of 1969. Still, they do merge as a three-part poem, unified in subject matter and tone, celebrating the heroism of seeing deeply and well.

The Poems of Marianne Moore (2003), a posthumous complete edition, with a few exceptions presents final versions of poems, and therefore the three do not appear there in order of their first publication. However, since the poems were written sequentially they are set side by side in the chronological edition.

I use the term "poetic sequence" as M. L. Rosenthal defined it for the modern period: "a group of lyric poems and passages, rarely uniform in pattern, which interact as an organic whole." The poetic sequence is hardly new but its emphatic disparity does seem to be a modern feature. For models of past centuries, I think of music: Bach's B Minor Mass, comprised of passages in unlike forms, attains a range of emotion: intensity of belief, gravity of death, joy of resurrection.

As for the theme, perception has been a major concern in poetry from time immemorial. The great poetic sequences in

Previously unpublished. Given as an address to the Associated Writing Programs Conference, February 2008.

the period we call modern rely on images of seeing to transform the world's evils, drawing them into aesthetic spheres. In *The Cantos* of Ezra Pound, the *periplum*, or seeing speaker, by attaining a new view of land from shipboard, rises to perceive present truths by traveling to the past and to other cultures. In Eliot's *The Waste Land* the prophet Tiresias, though blind, envisions salvation in a decadent society.

Those sequences, bound together by images of clear vision, are heirs to Emerson's notion of self as a "transparent eyeball": "I am nothing. I see all." From Emerson Whitman took one of the great organizing principles of his *Leaves of Grass*, forerunner of the modern poetic sequence, to create the speaker who declares: "I perceive," "I peeringly view from the top," "I observe," and "seeing, hearing, feeling are miracles."

In her early work, like the French Symbolists before her, Moore uses the artist's vision to penetrate beyond surface appearances. Moore writes in 1921 that a work of art "must be 'lit with piercing glances into the life of things,' / it must acknowledge the spiritual forces which have made it." And a year later, in "People's Surroundings," she contrasts the "cool sirs" of conventional vision with a deeper scrutiny, an "X-Ray-like inquisitive intensity."

Indeed, the process of obtaining knowledge by sight is realized in virtually all the poems of Marianne Moore that appear between January 1921 and June 1953. The figure of sight may be in the conversational opening of a poem ("you've seen a strawberry"), or may serve an emergent definition, as of the mind in "The Mind Is an Enchanting Thing" ("it's memory's eye"). Although its use is not overly apparent in many of the poems, seeing is present in all of them, and is fundamental to their structures and meaning. Moore is, of course, a poet of observation: the ubiquity of sight imagery tells us her concern is not what is observed but how.

Early and late, Moore had a predilection for the poetic sequence. "Pouters and Fantails," consisting of five independent poems, appeared in *Poetry* as early as 1915. In 1934 came the publication, again in *Poetry,* of "Imperious Ox, Imperial Dish," the overall title she gave to "The Buffalo" and "Nine Nectarines." Two years later, a sequence called "The Old Dominion," made up of "Virginia Britannia," "Bird-Witted," "Half-Deity," "Smooth Gnarled Crape Myrtle," and "The Pangolin," came out in England as part of a slim book, *The Pangolin and Other Poems*.

From the beginning, Moore concentrated on seeing things from multiple perspectives: the person who has seen the animal, how the animal behaves. In contemplating small objects and animals, Moore struggles through to an understanding of passion, the unity of the individual, courage, selflessness, the timeless values we cherish even under pressure. Her mode of seeing combines external and spiritual realities, examining them and at the same time cherishing a reverence for mystery. The sequence, "Part of a Poem, Part of a Novel, Part of a Play," displays Moore's ideal vision of a reality more coherent than ordinary perception.

In the sequence, the very word "hero" is echoed by *ee* and *o* sounds throughout. It is further bound together by repetitions of the essential words "hero," "see," "danger," "hope." Each of the poems has a central character, and each character is heroic in his way of seeing reality. The three are introduced in "The Steeple-Jack," set in a town in Maine. In it

> The hero, the student,
> the steeple-jack, each in his way,
> is at home.

The steeple-jack is C. J. Poole, whose name contains the pun on "seeing": C. (see) and Poole (sea/see). He performs heroic deeds in a town of contrasts. At the outset, all is calm:

> Dürer would have seen a reason for living
> in a town like this, with eight stranded whales
> to look at: with the sweet sea air coming into your
> house
> on a fine day, from water etched
> with waves as formal as the scales
> on a fish.
>
> One by one, in two's, in three's, the seagulls keep
> flying back and forth over the town clock,
> or sailing around the lighthouse without moving the
> wings—

> rising steadily with a slight
> > quiver of the body—or flock
> mewing where

The words "seen," "see," and "look" are used repeatedly in the first four stanzas, from the opening lines onward, emphasized by assonance. The assonance reaches its highest pitch in the third stanza:

> a sea the purple of the peacock's neck is
> > paled to a greenish azure as Dürer changed
> the pine green of the Tyrol to peacock blue and guinea
> gray. You can see a twenty-five-
> > pound lobster . . .

Both scene and chatty tone change in stanza four as to render the description of order an elaborate disguise. The scene is suddenly presented in imagery of natural violence:

> The
> whirlwind fife-and-drum of the storm bends the salt
> > marsh grass, disturbs stars in the sky and the
> star on the steeple; it is a privilege to see so
> much confusion . . .

The shift is reinforced by images of seeing. Gradually we become aware that the poet is using "sea" as a pun on "see." Its use enables her to reinforce musically the importance of "seeing" and the meaning of perception. The pun incarnates the process of "seeing" false appearances. "It is a privilege to see so much confusion," the speaker asserts bravely, though there are many indications of danger. And later we learn of the fear:

> This would be a fit haven for
> waifs, children, animals, prisoners,
> > and presidents who have repaid
> sin-driven
>
> senators by not thinking about them.

Or so it could be but for C. J. Poole, who places "danger signs by the church" while "gilding the solid-pointed star," which, we learn, is a visible, man-made manifestation of the mysterious quality of hope. "It could not be dangerous to be living / in a town like this, of simple people," the speaker asserts, but we know that it is dangerous, and that the people are hardly simple. Yet following the steeple-jack's example, they have the ability to live with confusion, distrusting perception and yet continually questioning what is real.

The title character of "The Student," introduced as Ambrose in "The Steeple-Jack," is, like C. J. Poole, faced with chaos, for "study is beset with dangers." And yet he is described as "patience personified,"

> a variety
> of hero, "patient
> of neglect and of reproach,"—who can "hold by
>
> himself."

The student is better than you and I, for

> he renders service when there is
> no reward, and is too reclusive for
> some things to touch
> him, not because he
> has no feeling but because he has so much.

The steeple-jack's hope recurs in "The Hero," presented now as patience that is required to live with mysteries we cannot fathom. Hope is that quality presented as "hope not being hope / until all ground for hope has / vanished." The hero of the title is "a decorous frock-coated Negro" who has a "sense of human dignity / and reverence for mystery, standing like the shadow / of the willow." He stands unlike the "sightseeing hobo" who would know everything she can. The hero knows that reality is not immediately accessible:

> He's not out
> seeing a sight but the rock
> crystal thing to see—the startling El Greco
> brimming with inner light—that
> covets nothing that it has let go. This then you may know
> as the hero.

Throughout her work, Moore is concerned with the heroic act of seeing "the rock / crystal thing to see." "The Steeple-Jack," "The Student," and "The Hero," all unalike in form, enact that way of seeing. She was to leave the form later and extol the seeing process in lyric poems. But considering these 1921 poems as a sequence can show forth her conviction, shared by many American poets of her time, that the faculty of seeing beneath and beyond is the most valuable thing we have.

Sylvia Plath and Yaddo

Sylvia Plath and Ted Hughes spent a little over two months at Yaddo, an artists' colony in Saratoga Springs, New York, in the autumn of 1959. There they lived and worked from September 10 until just before Thanksgiving, when they returned to her Wellesley home, soon to begin a long residence in England. It was at Yaddo that Sylvia Plath wrote the last poems in *The Colossus,* poems that marked a decisive change in her development as a woman and as a writer.

In "Sylvia Plath and Her Journals," Ted Hughes recalls that the Yaddo poems brought her from the first to the second phase of her work, from "death" to "birth": "the birth of her new creative self." He writes in that essay: "During the next three years she came to view this time as the turning point in her writing career, the point where her real writing began."

The "death" he recounts was her first failed suicide attempt in 1953, when she lay undiscovered in darkness for three days, and subsequently was subjected to unsuccessful electric shock therapy. The long process of rebuilding the self took place over the following years and, in the autumn of 1959, she perceived a new measure of her own being and moved into herself.

In terms of external events of her life that autumn, we know from her letters, from her mother's comments, and from Ted Hughes's recollections, that she learned she was pregnant (with her first child, Frieda, the girl she was to deliver in England the following April); she celebrated her twenty-seventh birthday with a cake and candles and *vin rosé;* she studied German; she devised, with her husband, exercises in incantation to change

Originally appeared in *Ariel Ascending,* edited by Paul Alexander (New York: Harper and Row, 1985).

the tone of her earlier descriptive poems (as in "Mussel Hunter at Rock Harbor") to a more immediate diction (as in "Mushrooms," which developed from the incantations).

Yaddo poems which displayed her new individuality are "Blue Moles," of two dead moles she and Hughes found on the Yaddo grounds; "The Manor Garden," in which she depicts the Yaddo landscape and foretells the birth of her first child; "The Colossus," based on a dream in which she was trying to reassemble a giant, shattered, stone Colossus; at least two sections of "Poem for a Birthday" ("Flute Notes from a Reedy Pond" and "The Stones"), both generated by her own birthday; "The Burnt-out Spa," which records the ruins of a health spa near Yaddo; "Mushrooms" and "Medallion." She wrote other poems during this productive visit, but did not include them in *The Colossus*. They are "Polly's Tree," referring to Polly Hanson, a poet who served as secretary to the director; "Yaddo: The Grand Manor," an observation of the mansion; "Private Ground" and "Dark Wood, Dark Water," both based on the Yaddo landscape.*

The dramatic change in her life and work occurred in a suitable place. Plath wrote in her West House studio, a room she described once as "low-ceilinged, painted white, with a cot, a rug, a huge, heavy darkwood table that I use as a typing and writing table with piles of room for papers and books." Of the Yaddo grounds, she told her mother: "I particularly love the scenic beauty of the estate: the rose gardens, goldfish pools, marble statuary everywhere, woodland walks, little lakes." Besides these pleasures, it is certain that she enjoyed the freedom of working undisturbed, in solitude, as well as being cared for as an artist, and meeting other artists as a colleague.

West House, the adjunct to the Yaddo mansion, has not changed considerably since 1959. When I first visited Yaddo in 1973, I found, on bookshelves just outside my West House stu-

---

*The information that these poems were written at Yaddo in autumn 1959 is from "Notes on the Chronological Order of Sylvia Plath's Poems," by Ted Hughes, in which the dates are approximate, and from the groupings, with exact dates, in Sylvia Plath, *The Collected Poems*, edited by Ted Hughes (New York: Harper and Row, 1981).

dio, Theodore Roethke's *The Waking* and Paul Radin's *African Folktales,* two books which were essential, respectively, to Plath's earlier and later work. Roethke's vision of the natural world—a cruel, terrifying, but fascinating realm—was close to Plath's view, and probably a powerful influence as well. Radin's book is filled with primitive ritual and tribal utterance, and its life-giving energy fires the celebratory voices of *Ariel.*

When I looked through the windows of the West House sitting room, I saw rows of white pines, junipers, blue spruce and Norwegian spruce trees. The white pine trunks resembled legs of a giant animal; leaves, insects, and small birds appeared distorted, as in the enlargements and diminutions found in Sylvia Plath's poems of the natural world—the "outsize hands" of "Blue Moles," the "archaic / Bones of the great trees" in "Dark Wood, Dark Water"—images which alter life to convey life with more accuracy.

On a subsequent visit to Yaddo I worked in West House again, this time in Sylvia Plath's studio. (The enormous bedroom that she and Ted Hughes had lived in is on the ground floor, near bookshelves and the sitting room with quarreled window panes.) My studio, on the top floor, had a terrace which overlooked a white pine tree with a branch that jutted toward me, bearing a starburst that changed into a mourning dove, into the limp hand of St. James the Less, a painting by El Greco I had just seen at the Hyde Collection in Glens Falls, not far from Yaddo. Objects seemed capable of change, at times because of the altering sunlight, and at other times because the imagination projected its fancies upon them during intense concentration, dressing them in idealized garb the way the eyes can transform a lover.

The marble statues, the Tiffany vases and metal sconces in West House, the stained-glass windows of the mansion are objects, which seem to flow from the imagination, and require little or no transformation. When writing about a fluted lantern, or a stereopticon with slides of the Alhambra, or trees seen through mullioned window panes, less transmutation is desirable or even possible. In Sylvia Plath's "Yaddo: The Grand Manor," a minor poem but one that captures the dreamlike estate, she writes:

> Indoors, Tiffany's phoenix rises
> Above the fireplace;
> Two carved sleighs
> Rest on orange plush near the newel post.

The improbable scene is real, as is the ending:

> The late guest
> Wakens, mornings, to a cobalt sky,
> A diamond-paned window,
> Zinc-white snow.

Sylvia Plath was a poet of keen observation and inquiry; even when images are distorted or information altered, it is done to convey a sharper, more penetrating truth. Often she combines her precise images with unusual verbs, and her lines are compressed to yield clusters of strong accents. However, when writing of Yaddo interiors, the strong verbs drop away and her skillful molding of images is lessened. It is as though she found that simply by recording the fantastic objects in the manor houses, rather than by analyzing or recreating, she could convey their being.

Occasionally this lack of meticulous precision freed her to develop ways of examining inner terrors, methods which were to become central to *Ariel*. Those devices have their roots in the Yaddo period. "The Manor Garden," a Yaddo landscape poem which looks toward the birth of her child, is far more successful than "Yaddo: The Grand Manor":

> The fountains are dry and the roses over.
> Incense of death. Your day approaches.
> The pears fatten like little buddhas.
> A blue mist is dragging the lake.
>
> You move through the era of fishes,
> The smug centuries of the pig—
> Head, toe and finger
> Come clear of the shadow. History
>
> Nourishes these broken flutings,
> These crowns of acanthus,
> And the crow settles her garments.
> You inherit white heather, a bee's wing,

Two suicides, the family wolves,
Hours of blankness. Some hard stars
Already yellow the heavens.
The spider on its own string

Crosses the lake. The worms
Quit their usual habitations.
The small birds converge, converge
With their gifts to a difficult borning.

The first line, seemingly surreal, actually has its basis in accurate observation: at Yaddo in autumn stone fountains have a bygone quality and the rose garden is bare. So, too, with the "blue mist," and once again the poet finds precisely the right verb for the lake image. The "broken flutings" and "crowns of acanthus" turn up in "The Colossus" addressed to the father as "Your fluted bones and acanthine hair." Actually, they are objects found among the stone and marble statuary she loved on the Yaddo ground.

This manner of observation has an interesting bearing on the imagery in *Ariel*. In "November Graveyard," an earlier poem, she shows a remarkable fidelity to nature in developing the graveyard metaphor of bare trees. In "Elm," a later poem, her images are associated but born of genuine observation, as though fantastic images have their place in reality and dreamlike objects are genuine, existing simultaneously with natural things.

In "The Manor Garden," she writes of the child growing in her surrounded by death, and by chilly, terrifying natural images. Those images of the physical universe lack their autonomy, being pressed to serve a human cause. Still, this poem is celebratory: the fetus is strong and alive ("Head, toe and finger / Come clear of the shadow"), and there is certainty about the birth, difficult though the borning may be. The woman, threatened by her past, is nevertheless sure of her unborn child's activity and strength ("Your day approaches" and "You move through the era of fishes"). Like many of Sylvia Plath's later poems, it is a work of fearful praise—a praise that may be even stronger for its implicit faith in life despite lurking terrors.

"Blue Moles" is another of the transitional Yaddo poems which exhibits this phase of her writing at its best. Its composition was preceded by "Private Ground," which she excluded from *The Colossus,* a poem considerably weaker for its discursiveness and lack of focus. In the last stanza of "Private Ground," however, she attempts what she achieves in "Blue Moles"—the unlikely identification between the speaker and dead creatures. All morning, the guest has been watching the handyman draining the goldfish ponds.

Then,

> I bend over this drained basin where the small fish
> Flex as the mud freezes.
> They glitter like eyes, and I collect them all.

In "Blue Moles," the stronger poem, she achieves that identification—an uneasy unity—with the wretched natural creatures:

(1)

> They're out of the dark's ragbag, these two
> Moles dead in the pebbled rut,
> Shapeless as flung gloves, a few feet apart—
> Blue suede a dog or fox has chewed.
> One, by himself, seemed pitiable enough,
> Little victim unearthed by some large creature
> From his orbit under the elm root.
> The second carcass makes a duel of the affair:
> Blind twins bitten by bad nature.

(2)

> Nightly the battle-shouts start up
> In the ear of the veteran, and again
> I enter the soft pelt of the mole.
> Light's death to them: they shrivel in it.
> They move through their mute rooms while I sleep,
> Palming the earth aside, grubbers
> After the fat children of root and rock.
> By day, only the topsoil heaves.
> Down there one is alone. . . .

In the first section, Plath presents, in hard, unsparing detail, two moles found dead, by the exigencies of a violent, natural order and observed in a stony grove at Yaddo. Later the observer finds an unexpected oneness with them ("I enter the soft pelt"), while preserving gingerly her own detachment ("while I sleep," "the topsoil heaves"). As in many of her nature poems, strong active verbs, compression, and crowded lines with heavy stresses and few light syllables convey her fascination with the victimized creatures, and also with the cruel natural world. Plath's probing moles, "palming the earth aside," are akin to her own passions for inquiry, information, fact. These night creatures, ill-fated, shriveling in light, suggesting human defeat and solitude, are more subtly images of the unconscious. Death and the unconscious are quietly linked here in a way that creativity itself emerges as a creature threatened by light. The striking effect of "Blue Moles," though, is the poet's excitement and amazement, qualities enforced by the heavily stressed lines. Although what she depicts is dead and cold, her passion and wonder epitomize vitality, and are further echoed in the music.

In "Mushrooms," another of the poems written during her Yaddo stay, Plath is so closely identified with the plants as to speak for them as "we." Again, they are objects that move at night:

> Overnight, very
> Whitely, discreetly,
> Very quietly
> Our toes, our noses
> Take hold on the loam,
> Acquire the air.
> Nobody sees us,
> Stops us, betrays us;
> The small grains make room.

In the last three stanzas, the mushrooms declare their triumph:

> We are shelves, we are
> Tables, we are meek,
> We are edible,
> Nudgers and shovers
> In spite of ourselves.
> Our kind multiplies:
> We shall by morning
> Inherit the earth.
> Our foot's in the door.

"Mushrooms," written November 13 and one of the last poems she wrote at Yaddo, looks toward the new mode in which she speaks for the person or object she contemplates. It prefigures the liberating voices of *Ariel*. Here, though, the identification is with a force that is energetic but frightening in its aggression. The human character of the vegetable mushrooms seems evident in the language: "discreetly," "our toes, our noses," "nudgers and shovers." The poet is writing of a cold physical universe but the prevailing tone is, again, astonishment.

According to Ted Hughes, "The Colossus" and several sections of "Poem for a Birthday," a poem written on November 4, follow Plath's dream of trying to assemble a shattered stone giant.

If a poet's use of imagery were ever predictable, it might be expected that Plath would dwell on stone images at the Yaddo estate. In fact, stones are everywhere in that place: stone fountains, stone pedestals, the fieldstone towers of West House, the turreted sandstone mansion with its stone terrace, the stone arch to a stately rose garden, "the rock garden" where water streams from a pile of moss-covered black rocks and falls into a pool enclosed by stones on ground where fallen pine needles have turned amber in the sunlight, the gravestones of Spenser Trask and his wife, Katrina, who willed their estate to artists.

Nearly all of Plath's Yaddo poems incorporate images of stones, often associated with dead creatures. The dead moles are seen "neutral as the stones"; "The Manor Garden" begins with an image of dry stone fountains and an ambience of death; in "Private Ground," the goldfish perish in drained stone basins; in "Medallion," the poet, in silent wonder, examines a dead snake, turns it in the light and recalls: "When I split a rock one time / The garnet bits burned like that." And, of course, the overwhelming figure of the broken stone Colossus, her title poem for her first collection of poems, evokes the concluding statement: "No longer do I listen for the scrape of a keel / On the blank stones of the landing."

All things considered, it is not surprising that she dreamed of the demolished Colossus while she lived among the stones at Yaddo. Most of all, her father's actual gravestone had affected her deeply when she had visited it in Azalea Path, Winthrop, Massachusetts, on March 9 of that year. She had written:

> Three graveyards separated by streets, all made within the last fifty years or so, ugly crude black stones, headstones together, as if the dead were sleeping head to head in a poorhouse. In the third yard, on a flat grassy area looking across a sallow barren stretch to rows of wooden tenements I found the flat stone: *Otto E. Plath: 1885–1940.* Right beside the path, where it would be walked over. Felt cheated. My temptation to dig him up. To prove he existed and really was dead.

This reflection is quoted in *The Collected Poems,* in a note to "Electra on the Azalea Path," a poem she excluded from *The Colossus.* In it, she links her father's death with her own longing for extinction, and ends with a hard-edged but pitiable cry of self-loathing: "O pardon the one who knocks for pardon at / Your gate, father—your hound-bitch, daughter, friend. / It was my love that did us both to death." Pitiable though it may be, excessive emotion renders it less believable than her impious attitude which follows, especially in "The Colossus."

In "Sylvia Plath and Her Journals," Ted Hughes provides a gloss on the father in "The Colossus" when he writes of her Ouija board fascination in the late 1950s, when agents would bring words from an underworld Prince Otto (her father's name). Hughes writes:

> When she pressed for a more personal communication, she would be told that Prince Otto could not speak to her directly, because he was under orders from the Colossus. And when she pressed for an audience with The Colossus, they would say he was inaccessible.

In "Ouija" and in "Electra on the Azalea Path," both preceding the composition of "The Colossus," the male figures are powerful and remote: "a chilly god, a god of shades" in the earlier "Ouija," and a loved dead father in the later poem.

In the light of the events that informed the earlier poems, it does seem clear that "The Colossus" represents a turning point in her poems about the father. It reveals the changes in her gods and in what she spoke of as her "death," the failed suicide attempt of 1953. After "The Colossus," those themes are objectified, developed presentatively, with minimal description. "The Colossus" itself exhibits a rather sassy, defiant attitude toward the stone ruins addressed as father. Where "Ouija" called forth a god, "The Colossus" portrays another creature entirely: "Perhaps you consider yourself an oracle, / Mouthpiece of the dead, or of some god or other." Most striking are the ironic, mock-heroic effects; antithetical to the damaged stone mass, the speaker performs small, domestic labors: "Scaling little ladders with gluepots and pails of Lysol / I crawl like an ant in mourning / Over the weedy acres of your brow . . ."

"The Colossus" is a better poem than "Electra on the Azalea Path" because of its frankly unsentimental view, enforced by withheld emotion and by a preposterous, wildly humorous central image. If the massive image here is inaccessible, like the earlier figures, the speaker is irreverent, weary of trying to mend the immense stone ruins. Plath is still very far from her outcry of 1962, "Daddy, daddy, you bastard, I'm through." She is, however, at this point, turning from the stone wreckage of another being to the ruins of her own. The movement is vital, for it indicates her wish to leave death—her father's actual death and her own dramatized death—for new life. That transformation took place among the stones of Yaddo in the fall of 1959.

Accordingly "The Stones" is the final poem of the sequence "Poem for a Birthday," written at Yaddo, and it carries over the ruins of "The Colossus." In "The Stones," though, the scene is a hospital city "where men are mended," and the speaker is one who has lived in fragments, and is now reborn. The entire sequence is a departure from her concern with the cruel natural world and its victimized creatures. It leaves the received mythology of the earlier poems: "The wingy myths won't tug at us anymore," she writes, in "Flute Notes from a Reedy Pond," another poem in the sequence. "The Stones" is the seventh, and last:

> This is the city where men are mended.
> I lie on a great anvil.
> The flat blue sky-circle

Flew off like the hat of a doll
When I fell out of the light. I entered
The stomach of indifference, the wordless cupboard.

. . . .

This is the after-hell: I see the light.
A wind unstoppers the chamber
Of the ear, old worrier.

Water mollifies the flint lip,
And daylight lays its sameness on the wall.
The grafters are cheerful,

Heating the pincers, hoisting the delicate hammers.
A current agitates the wires
Volt upon volt. Catgut stitches my fissures . . . .

Ted Hughes sees this poem as the culmination of her rebuilding a new self out of her father's "ruins," her primary work
up to age twenty-seven. He writes of "The Stones": "It is the birth
of her real poetic voice, but it is the rebirth of herself. That
poem encapsulates, with literal details, her 'death,' her treat-
ment, and her slow, buried recovery."

In this poem she writes in the well-known voice of *Ariel*, re-
placing the earlier narrative, expository utterance with stark,
passionate lines which cry out for life in the midst of death. It
shows a great leap from her poems of the cold natural universe.
"The Stones" has an associative movement built on images she
has considered and used for some years in a tone of Romantic
wonder. "The Stones" begins with the repair of her fallen self,
her earlier "death," the stillness broken only by her voice "in a
quarry of silences." It progresses in a rapid jerky manner, the
passionate outcries held in check by her skillful use of terza
rima, the form of many of the Yaddo poems, and done to technical perfection in "Medallion." In "The Stones," the work of
mending is given, image by image: "The jewelmaster drives his
chisel to pry / Open one stone eye." Then the light that was
"death" to the moles, as well as the speaker, is painfully manifest:
"This is the after-hell: I see the light." The senses are opened,
delicately but causing torment. The "current" is a healing one;
the catgut stitches are benign.

She writes with fierce irony but with praise, for a hospital that will substitute human qualities—hearts, eyes—for the ruins of a toppled being. "The Stones" is a poem of hard praise for life:

> Love is the bone and sinew of my curse.
> The vase, reconstructed, houses
> The elusive rose.

That life, however anguished, is the inevitable goal, the outcome of her passionate inquiry into tormented existence around her. The inquiry dazzles her into knowing she will survive in any way she can. "I shall be good as new" is her conclusion, her solemn promise.

Orient Expressed

From Lu Chi to Imagism

However varied their styles, poets writing in English today still rely on the early twentieth-century imagist principles of clarity, directness, presentative images, and rhythm based on cadences. Although imagism, revolutionary in its time, gathered force from several classical traditions, Chinese poetry was at the forefront.

The continued vitality of classic Chinese poetry is the impact of Sam Hamill's collection. It contains beautiful versions by more than sixty poets, from the *Shih Ching,* or "Poetry Classic" (1200–600 B.C.E.) through the eighth-century masters, Tu Fu, Li Po, and Wang Wei, to the sixteenth-century poet, Wang Yang-ming.

As W. S. Merwin writes in his elegant introduction, Sam Hamill's translations stand in a long tradition of classic Chinese poetry translations, notably Arthur Waley's *170 Chinese Poems* of 1918. He adds: "Sam Hamill's work, like Waley's, represents a lifetime's devotion to the classic originals, which survived in a long, subtle, intricate current."

Earlier than Waley's work, Ezra Pound's slim book *Cathay* (1915) was a landmark in poetry as well as in translation. Pound's contemporaries valued the tactile images and the musical freedom based on the concurrence of sounds, rather than on rhyme and fixed stress counts. Still, his versions were marred by inaccuracies (such as referring to the "River Kiang" as though

This piece is expanded from one that appeared in *The Nation,* vol. 271, no. 13 (Oct. 30, 2000), originally published as a review of two books: *Crossing the Yellow River: Three Hundred Poems from the Chinese,* translated and introduced by Sam Hamill, preface by W. S. Merwin, and *Lu Chi's Wen Fu: The Art of Writing,* translated by Sam Hamill.

the river had a name, when actually the word "kiang" means river). "The Chinese Written Character as a Medium for Poetry," an essay written by Ernest Fenollosa and edited by Pound, introduced a new poetic method in which clusters of images and ideas (similar to a Chinese written character) would take the place of the old logic and sequence of European poetics.

I don't read Chinese. I believe, though, that Sam Hamill has reached new heights in rendering these versions. Following Pound's directness and musical freedom, he returns to form, but in a far more natural way than did Pound's Georgian predecessors. For example, in translating the work of Tu Fu (712–70) Hamill observes the couplet that follows syntactical parallelism, as in "the palace walls will divide us / and clouds will bury the hills" ("Taking Leave of Two Officials"). Rightly the tone supersedes regularity of meter and rhyme, but in his approximation of original forms he uses assonance, consonance, and near rhyme.

The poems are radiant. "Taking Leave of a Friend," by Li Po (701–62), reads in its entirety:

> Green mountains rise to the north;
> white water rolls past the eastern city.
>
> Once it has been uprooted,
> the tumblewood travels forever.
>
> Drifting clouds like a wanderer's mind;
> sunset, like the heart of your old friend.
>
> We turn, pause, look back and wave.
> Even our ponies look back and whine.

Li Po evokes the torment of emotional ambivalence with startling truth. The first two couplets contain natural images in motion, capturing the wanderer's intention: mountains that rise, water that rolls, tumbleweed that travels. The second set of couplets present images of fixity that also imply the doom of mortality. He is compelled to roam and he is attached—as are we all.

Here is the title poem of this collection, "Crossing the Yellow River," by Wang Wei (701–61):

A little boat on the great river
whose waves reach the end of the sky—

suddenly a great city, ten thousand
houses dividing sky from wave.

Between the towns there are
hemp and mulberry trees in the wilds.

Look back on the old country:
wide waters; clouds; and rising mist.

The metaphor, crossing the river, implies boundaries between present and past, change and habit, youth and the sense of aging (the latter prevalent in this anthology). By and large, the poets here attempt not the big emotion, which by itself can be intimidating, but the little cracks in that emotion. They deal with innuendoes, with truth relayed as it is in common speech, through bits of information, through sudden juxtapositions, through offhand observations of nature. From T. S. Eliot and Marianne Moore down to the present, this kind of emotional accounting prevails: I think immediately of poems such as Moore's "The Paper Nautilus," Eliot's "Preludes," Philip Levine's "Milkweed," and Karl Kirchwey's "In Transit," among many others.

Li Ch'ing-chao (1084?–1151) is one of the book's few poets known to be a woman. According to Sam Hamill's Notes on the Poets, she was one of China's greatest and also "an influential critic of her age." "To the Tune: Boat of Stars" brings back to me Ezra Pound's remarkable adaptation of Li Po's "The River Merchant's Wife." Her poem begins:

Spring after spring, I sat before my mirror.
Now I tire of braiding plum buds in my hair.

I've gone another year without you,
shuddering with each letter.

Like the speakers of the early Anglo-Saxon poems, such as "Wulf and Eadwacer" and "The Wife's Lament," the personae often are women, but the author is unknown. The poems are brief, even slight, but their wit leaves room for growth. Here, for instance, is "A Smile":

In this house without walls on a hill,
the four winds touch our faces.

If they blow open your robe of gauze,
I'll try to hide my smile.

Hamill's revised translation of Lu Chi's *Wen Fu: The Art of Writing*, a fourth-century *ars poetica*, reveals practices that are valuable for our time. More than a handbook, it counsels the mind and the spirit, which are all of a piece with style in Confucian Chinese thought. From Lu Chi's poetic treatise come these important maxims:

As infinite as space, good work
joins earth to heaven

and

Although each form is different, each opposes evil:
and none grants a writer licence.

Language must speak from its essence to articulate reason:
verbosity indicates lack of virtue.

Some of Lu Chi's injunctions are familiar ground rules:

Only through writing and then revising and revising
may one gain the necessary insight.

Others are subtle but immensely meaningful:

Past and present commingle:
Eternity in a single blink of an eye!

Emotion and reason are not two different things;
every shift in feeling must be read.

The "wen" of *Wen Fu* means literary arts. In Confucian China, Hamill tells us, writing was inseparable from morality in that truth meant naming things. The "fu" is the form, whose syntactic parallelism strikes this listener as having affinities with passages in the Hebrew Bible, notably the Song of Songs.

As in the poetry anthology, Sam Hamill's translation is superb. He conveys profound ideas and intricate images with simplicity, naturalness, and directness. The *Wen Fu* has appeared in other translations. When I was a child trying to write poetry, I was given for my birthday a desk dictionary and the Bollingen edition of E. R. Hughes's Lu Chi's *Wen Fu, A.D. 302,* which includes the document's history as well as a translation. The giver was my "Uncle Ted," E. McKnight Kauffer, who I've written about earlier in this essay collection. I had asked him what books I might read in the hope of becoming a writer, and he thought of the Bollingen edition, which he designed. Both books became constant companions, though the Hughes translation of *Wen Fu* was nothing short of ponderous. And so I was especially grateful for Sam Hamill's version. His prose is a breeze.

Sam Hamill, founding editor of Copper Canyon Press, is the author of more than thirty books. The latest and best of his eleven poetry collections is *Gratitude* (1998). In "Discovering the Artist Within," he tells a disconcerting but lifting story of how he came to poetry. Orphaned at the age of two, adopted, then beaten and sexually molested, he grew up to commit unlawful acts. Throughout his difficult early adulthood, though, he held to his literary talent as to a life raft. Among the contemporary poets whose work saved him and his writing were the Beat poets, Gary Snyder, and especially Kenneth Rexroth, whose *One Hundred Poems from the Chinese* Hamill thanks in his new volume.

It was from Rexroth he learned the discipline poetry required. Then, three years in Japan, two in the U.S. Marine Corps, and one on a fellowship added to his expertise as an Asian linguist as well as to his Zen practice.

Devotion aside, these books will endure. Their tone is a combination of zest, generosity, and humility. "We are fortunate to live during the greatest time for poetry since the T'ang Dynasty," Hamill writes in his introduction to *Crossing the River,* aware that the classic Chinese poems are the essence of today's practice. His humility is apparent from the last sentence of his introduction: "I sit at the feet of the great old masters of my tradition not only to be in a position to pass on their many wonderful gifts, but to pay homage while in the very act of nourishing, sustaining and enhancing my own life." It is an impassioned stance for our casual age, but after reading the two books I know that every word of his credo is true.

Stephen Sondheim, Dramatic Poet

Stephen Sondheim's lyrics have been celebrated for bringing fresh air to the musical theater. My persuasion is that his words transcend their musical and dramatic settings and stand alone as poems. Unfortunately, poets and critics have been hard put to discover that because there is no collection of his lyrics in the bookstores. There are editions that include texts and production photographs, but only of four Sondheim shows. To examine his words, serious readers must collate the libretto inserts they have fished out of their CD, LP, and cassette albums (and not all of them are so equipped), or else must transcribe the tapes they have copied with loving care, intuiting punctuation and line breaks, as I do now. But never mind. It is well worth it. Composing the words and music for most of his shows since the late 1950s, Sondheim has created songs that are intelligent, graceful and agile. He is a satirist with an ear for street talk, a humorist who ranges from urbane wit to broad comedy:

> I've got those
> "God-why-don't-you-love-me-
> oh-you-do-I'll-see-you-later"
> Blues
> —"Buddy's Blues," *Follies*

> Sweetheart, lover,
> Could I recover,
> Give up the joys I have known?
> Not to fetch your pills again

This essay first appeared in *The Poetry of Song,* edited by George Robert Minkoff and J. D. McClatchy (New York: Poetry Society of America, 1992).

Every day at five,
Not to give those dinners for ten
Elderly men
From the U.N.—
How could I survive?
                    —"Could I Leave You?" *Follies*

He has a keen sensitivity to social evil, such as nineteenth-century imperialism:

The practical bird,
Having no tree of its own,
Borrows another's.
                    —*Pacific Overtures*

Besides the humor, he risks complex ideas that in lesser hands would burden the musical settings. Although a lyric usually expresses one emotion or two contrasting ones, Sondheim's characters sing of several simultaneous feelings, often contradicting themselves, or thinking aloud. He writes flowing songs in which two or more singers melodiously embody conflicting points of view. And most notably, he offers a tough moral wisdom that is hard-edged, unsentimental, sane:

I chose, and my world was shaken—
So what?
The choice may have been mistaken,
The choosing was not.
You have to move on.
            —"Move On," *Sunday in the Park with George*

Somebody know me too well.
Somebody pull me up short
And put me through hell and give me support
For being alive.
                    —"Being Alive," *Company*

There won't be trumpets or bolts of fire
To say he's coming.
No Roman candles, no angels' choir.
No sound of distant drumming.
    —"There Won't be Trumpets," *Anyone Can Whistle*

But depth alone is not art. The question of whether his lyrics are poetry requires that we hear them also in their musical and dramatic contexts. To regard them in this way does not diminish them as poems any more than it would diminish Shakespeare's "Dirge" from *Cymbeline*, which was written to be sung rather than recited. And incidentally, as if in affirmation of this principle, Sondheim has composed an elegant setting for "Dirge" ("Fear No More"); it is heard in *The Frogs*, his musical drama based on Aristophanes' play.

Stephen Sondheim writes in the best tradition of the kind of lyric that had its flowering in England between 1588 and 1632. Of the Elizabethan lyric, W. H. Auden wrote: "Good composers chose good poems to be set, and good poets were glad to write verses for them." Poems by, for example, John Donne, Ben Jonson, and Thomas Campion have their own poetic form and also fit the music with no distortion of the natural accent. Of the dramatic lyric, Shakespeare is the model in English literature: his songs have their own poetic form; they were written to be sung and to fit their dramatic contexts: In *Twelfth Night*, for example, Feste sings "Come Away, Death," a song that adumbrates the Duke's self-love by exaggerating romantic feeling. I cite these examples not as comparisons, but as standards for considering the work at hand. The point is that according to these criteria, Sondheim's songs rank extremely high. They contain conversational hesitations, and they fit their musical gloves with little or no violation of their spoken accents: "Crazy business this, this life we live in" (*Follies*); "Flecks of light [pause] and dark" (*Sunday in the Park with George*); "So there's hell to pay" (*Merrily We Roll Along*); "It's 'I do!' and 'You don't!' and 'Nobody said that!' and 'Who brought the subject up first!'" (*Company*).

Many of Sondheim's lyrics have their own received forms. For example, the beautiful haiku debate, "Poems," from *Pacific Overtures:*

> Rain glistening
> On the silver birch
> Like my lady's tears.
> (Your turn.)

Haze hovering
Like the whisper of the silk
As my lady kneels.
(Your turn.)

Dawn flickering,
Tracing shadows of the pines
On my lady sleeping.
(Your turn.)

Another of the formal poems is "Echo Song," a scheme that calls for a line whose last syllables are repeated in a second line spoken by another character:

"I hear my heart say,
Let him live with me!"
(Live with me,
live with me!)
(Does he want me—
Does he!)
—*A Funny Thing Happened on the Way to the Forum*

Still another is a dramatic monologue, "Someone in a Tree," which is heard as a madrigal in *Pacific Overtures*. The song follows a remark that since there were no witnesses to an exploitative foreign treaty signed on March 31, 1854, forcing Japan to trade with the West, there can be no Japanese version of what happened. In the song, a local man confesses that when he was ten he climbed a tree and peered at men who gathered inside a "treaty house": "They kept drinking cups of tea, / They kept sitting on the floor." Another resident discloses that he hid under floorboards, and heard the men shout, arguing over law: "First I heard a creak and a thump, / Then I heard a clink." Most remarkably, Sondheim presents the scene entirely in first-hand, vivid details, and haltingly, as in the memory process. Only toward the end of the lyric does he show the historic import of what the singers had observed. As in many of Sondheim's lyrics, the power is not in what is told but in the silences.

Sondheim's achievement, though, is not as a poet in the theater but as a dramatic poet. His art is in writing lyrics that reveal situation and character. That is apparent in what I believe to be his masterpiece, *Sweeney Todd, the Demon Barber of Fleet Street*. At their best, the songs evoke horror, rather than present it, by the placement of words in the dramatic action. Like Ophelia's mad songs, they appear incongruously, unexpectedly. For example, the ballad "Nothing's Gonna Harm You" is begun by Tobias, the young assistant to Mrs. Lovett. In it, he swears devotion to the older woman, not yet fully realizing that she has been baking freshly slaughtered people in her pies to please Sweeney, the man she loves. A further irony is that she joins in the affectionate song, although she is soon to lock Tobias in the macabre bakehouse. The music swells; the lyrics are tender:

> Nothing's gonna harm you
> No, sir,
> Not while I'm around.
>
> Demons are prowling
> Everywhere
> Nowadays.
> I'll send 'em howling,
> I don't care—
> I got ways.
> Others can desert you—
> Not to worry—
> Whistle, I'll be there.

As in that song, Sondheim frequently blends high romantic music with lyrics that, in their dramatic contexts, show torment, ambivalence, or naiveté. There is, for instance, "Unworthy of Your Love," from *Assassins,* sung by a hopeful killer and his obsessive love. Or, more subtly, "Too Many Mornings," which has the sound of a love song but the words of a man becoming aware of a painful inner void. In *Sweeney Todd,* the billowing music and sweet words unveil a grim plot: Sweeney, the barber, vows vengeance on a corrupt judge and his beadle who, years before, had deported him, raped his wife, and abducted his daughter. In one of the songs, "Johanna," several characters sing harmoniously of discordant motivations. And many of the songs are so delicate as to heighten the dread, as when the beadle sings to the lustful judge:

When a girl's emergent.
Probably it's urgent
you defer to her gentility,
my lord.
Ladies in their sensitivities,
my lord,
Have a fragile sensibility.

And when Sweeney and the judge sing "Pretty Women," a marvelous duet whose lines, in falling rhythm, are set against the "rising" notes of a waltz:

Pretty women . . .
Fascinating . . .
Sipping coffee,
Dancing . . .
Pretty women
Are a wonder.
Pretty women . . .

Sweeney Todd is more direct, and consequently less satiric, than Sondheim's other social dramas. Its force is in the central character, the deranged barber: Sweeney's songs reveal a perception of evil so intense as to belong to us all, and to pervade our world as well:

There's a hole in the world
Like a great black pit
And it's filled with people
Who are filled with shit . . .

Its virtues distinguish his work as a whole, showing his genius as a lyricist and as a dramatic poet. They show his supreme fictional technique of creating songs whose speakers are unaware of their motivations and deepest desires. In some dramas, that ignorance has evil consequences; in others, tragic effects. In all, the lapsed knowledge makes us uncomfortable because it reminds us of ourselves. That achievement is in the mode of great tragedy. In fact, I would not be surprised if, one day, a contemporary tragedy were to come out of the musical theater, the work of this superb dramatic poet, Stephen Sondheim.

Léonie Adams

Although the work of Léonie Adams has been consigned to rare book rooms in libraries, her books, *Those Not Elect* (1925) and *High Falcon* (1929), which are not easily found now, flourished in their time. Born in New York, a graduate of Barnard, she won a "traveling fellowship" from the Guggenheim Foundation and lived in Europe from 1928 through 1930. In 1948–49 she was Consultant in Poetry to the Library of Congress; in 1954 she was, with Louise Bogan, winner of a Bollingen Prize for her *Poems: A Selection*. In 1959 and again in 1974, she received the Fellowship of The Academy of American Poets.

At first, and only at first, I was troubled by her diction. Published in a decade that received *The Waste Land, Harmonium,* and Moore's *Observations,* besides Dickinson's posthumous *Further Poems,* Adams's books had seemed to lack colloquial vigor. Indeed, at times her archaic inversions seem purposeless:

> Now the rich cherry whose sleek wood
> And top with silver petals traced,
> Like a strict box its gems encased,
> Has split from out that cunning lid . . .
> —"Country Summer"

> Death to the lady said
> While she to dancing-measures still
> Would move, while beauties on her lay . . .
> —"Death and the Lady"

First published in *Poetry Pilot,* The Academy of American Poets (Spring 1995).

Because of that, it took me a while to hear the music, which, when heard, drew me to her true achievement—a remarkable grasp of ambivalence and irony as basic to the human condition—the heart's lament, the heart's joy. Her music provides the naturalness that displays her wisdom.

> The moon above the milky field
> Gleaning moves her one slant light,
> The wind weeps from the cloud:
> Then, weeping wind, unshroud
> Pale Cassiopeia, blow
> The true-swung pole-lamp bright.
> To this room a midnight's come
> Which speaks but with the beating clock,
> While on glistening paws the mouse
> Creeps night-master of the house.
>
> "Night Piece"

Here and elsewhere, the cadences display words for their sounds and connotations. Lines are fluid. Never does she use meter and rhyme in such a way as to distort speech rhythms.

To be sure, often her subject is music:

> This measure was a measure to my mind,
> Still musical through the unlikely hush.
> The cold goes wide as doors, and in will
>   come
> Those notes of May set ringing through the
>   brush,
> Where every voice by natural law is dumb.
>
> "This Measure"

She writes in set forms, favoring rhymed stanzas of iambic pentameter. Frequently, she goes to medieval ballads and carols for form, as in her "Death and the Lady," "Lullaby," and "The Mount," and for subject matter:

> In coming to the feast I found
> A venerable silver-throated horn,
> Which were I brave enough to sound,
> Then all as from that moment born

Would breathe the honey of this clime,
And three times merry in their time,
Would praise the virtue of that horn.

"The Horn"

I began to realize her concern for the music of poetry when I became her student at Columbia University's School of General Studies. There she spoke often of prosody, and especially of variations possible in metrical patterns. "In a good poem, there is only one way to read a line," she asserted. Reading students' poems, she would ask: "Where do you really want the stresses in this line?" or "How do you want me to read this?" Once, clutching a worn black velvet hat on her desk, she declared: "Wyatt would *never* have done this!" On another occasion, barely audible, she proclaimed: "Only after you master the placement of stresses and light syllables, will you speak with authority."

She spoke excitedly of the well-observed image, whose accuracy was fundamental to her own poetry. For example, a startling poem, "The Bell Tower," links the human voice to one of the structures she had seen in Europe:

And first the sound must gather in deep bronze,
Till, rarer than ice, purer than a bubble of gold,
It fill the sky to beat on an airy shell.

For Adams, exactness was fidelity to perception, though perception is various. I remember speaking with her about theories of a physicist, Conant, who rejected either/or hypotheses for discoveries of truth that were subjectively based, and built on the variable relationships between perceiver and perceived. "Language itself is untidy. The only accuracy is one's own," I remember her saying. That kind of subjective precision is evident at the close of "Country Summer":

All stars stand close in summer air,
And tremble, and look mild as amber;
When wicks are lighted in the chamber
You might say stars were settling there.

And these rich-bodied hours of our delight
Show like a moth-wing's substance when the
                                            fall
Of confine-loosing, blue unending night
Extracts the spirit of this temporal
So space can pierce the crevice wide
                                            between
Fast hearts, skies deep-descended
                                            intervene.

Adams, who wrote with vatic immediacy, was a quiet-spoken person. As her student, I was intrigued by her combination of shyness and bold curiosity. I observed her eyes, nearly covered by bangs, darting continually around the classroom. Her devotion to poetry was remarkable. With the very young, she would spend conference hours teasing out the truth of experience— the bridge lights, the long walk, the response to a good reading. Not long before I met her, she had been widowed by her beloved William Troy, a writer and essayist on the modern novel. When we were friends, in the mid-1960s, she lived alone in a Chelsea Hotel suite littered with manuscripts of students and friends. These she read every night of her life.

One evening she arrived late to our conference hour, an unusual event for Adams. Tired and somewhat strained, her speech slower than usual, she said her late husband's sister, a nun under strict orders, had been granted permission to visit her. In those pre–Vatican II days, her sister-in-law had been forbidden to attend the funeral of Troy, a lapsed Catholic. Afterward, the nun was allowed a brief reunion with Adams, the first visit in some years. "I couldn't see her for long," Adams said, explaining that she had been asked suddenly to judge manuscripts for a poetry contest. Another poet had declined at the last minute, and Adams had offered to carry out the task. "These obligations seem arbitrary, and even ill-considered," Adams said. "But, well, she has her rules and I have mine."

I remember our walks on the Columbia campus, Léonie Adams chatting about friends, vignettes, and daily occurrences. Thinking of her poetry's awe, I had expected her, instead, to extol the new buds in spring, or to celebrate a Hudson River sunset. In her poems there are few observations of common life, and virtually no casual phrases. Instead, she strikes dread, reverence, terror, tirelessly exploring the natural world, and, at the same time, intimates mysteries beyond it. I remember most her contrasts: modesty and passion; fierce dedication and gentle humor; privacy and concern for others.

I know I will always hear her music, as in the poem "Lullaby," a surprising, tender, and ironic dirge for an elderly man.

> Hush, lullay,
> Your treasures all
> Encrust with rust.
> Your trinket pleasures
> Fall
> To dust.
> Beneath the sapphire arch
> Upon the grassy floor
> Is nothing more
> To hold,
> And play is ever old.
> Your eyes
> In sleepy fever gleam,
> Your lids droop
> To their dream.
> You wander late alone,
> The flesh frets on the bone,
> Your love fails
> In your breast.
> Here is the pillow.
> Rest.
>
> "Lullaby"

War Requiem

The Wild Card: Selected Poems, Early and Late. By Karl Shapiro, edited by Stanley Kunitz and David Ignatow.

Mid-twentieth-century events may be history but in art they have stayed new, animating films, music, and drama. In poetry, Karl Shapiro wrote powerfully of "the good war," and his vision is ready for a new generation as well. His book of selected poems (1942–92) is blessed to have distinguished editors, Stanley Kunitz and David Ignatow, and M. L. Rosenthal as author of the introduction.

The early poems, represented well in anthologies, grow out of an American post-Depression liberalism that was to marshal itself against the Axis powers in World War II. In "Death of Emma Goldman" Shapiro celebrates the anarchist as a neglected hero ("Dark conscience of the family"), and in "University" he assails racism:

> To hurt the Negro and avoid the Jew
> Is the curriculum . . .

"Buick," an erotic song to the American automobile, is actually a savage attack on American materialism:

> Leaning and laughing, my warm-hearted
> beauty, you ride, you ride,
> You tack on the curves with parabola
> speed and a kiss of goodbye.

and the poet's sharp satire leads to darker observations:

First published in *The Nation,* vol. 268, no. 4 (Feb. 1, 1999).

But how alien you are from the booming
  belts of your birth and the smoke
Where you turned on the stinging lathes
  of Detroit and Lansing at night . . .

Born in 1913, Shapiro gained recognition in his thirties. He won the Pulitzer Prize in 1945 and the Bollingen Prize in 1969. He was poetry consultant to the Library of Congress and editor of *Poetry*. Earlier, when his first book came out (*Person, Place, and Thing*, in 1942), he was serving with the Army in the South Pacific during World War II.

There and in *V-Letter and Other Poems* (1944), Shapiro is engulfed by war, fearful, unable to sleep for the "small burr of the bombers in our ear." War is "the vacuum of Hell, / The mouth of blood, the ocean's ragged jaw."

For him, the war crushes individuality. In "Sunday: New Guinea" Shapiro hears the bugle sounding "the measured calls to prayers" and confesses,

I long for our disheveled Sundays home,
Breakfast, the comics, news of latest crimes,
Talk without reference, and palindromes,
Sleep and the Philharmonic and the ponderous *Times*.

And in "Christmas Eve: Australia," Shapiro sees "quizzical soldiers" who are

sick of causes and the tremendous blame
curse lightly and pronounce your serious name.

Even the title, *V-Letter* (the precursor of our modern airmail letter-and-envelope) speaks of war's harsh denials. The title poem is a V-letter to his beloved:

I love you first because you wait, because
For your own sake, I cannot write
Beyond these words. I love you for these words
That sting and creep like insects and leave filth.

Early and late, Shapiro's poetry is exciting for its range of tone. Using conventional metrics, he plays the wild card with fresh language that is still alive. In "Elegy for a Dead Soldier," he rails against those who place statistics above the one killed, angrily comparing the dead victim to living hypocrites:

> Above all else he loathed the homily,
> The slogan and the ad. He paid his bill,
> But not for Congressmen at Bunker Hill.
> Ideals were few and those there were not made
> For conversation.

As early as *Person, Place, and Thing*, he combines antipatriotism, as in "Conscription Camp":

> We hawk and spit; our flag walks through
>   the air
> Breathing hysteria thickly in each face

with lyrical balladry, as in the beautiful "Nostalgia":

> My soul stands at the window of my room,
>   And I ten thousand miles away;
> My days are filled with Ocean's sound of
>   doom,
>   Salt and cloud and the bitter spray
> *Let the wind blow, for many a man shall*
>   *die.*

And later, in the prose poems of *The Bourgeois Poet* (1964), his tone shifts from mockery to prophetic warning:

> My century that boils history to a pulp for newspaper, my century of the million-dollar portrait, century of the decipherment of Linear B and the old scrolls, century of the dream of penultimate man . . . century of the turning-point of time, the human wolf pack and the killing light.

Fresh as their language is to us now, Shapiro's poems require a historical context to be apprehended fully. His work recalls that of Randall Jarrell, an airman, his senior by only one year. Both are obsessed with unending sounds of guns and bombers. In "Full Moon: New Guinea," Shapiro advises, during a long night of fear, "Breathe and wait, / The bombs are falling darkly for our fate." In Jarrell's "A Field Hospital," a soldier cries, "the shotguns stammer in my head. / I lie in my own bed."

Both share the human responsibility war's routines would deny. In "The Gun," Shapiro addresses his weapon:

> I absolve from your name
> The exaction of murder, my gun. It is I who have killed.
> It is I whose enjoyment of horror is fine and fulfilled.
> You are only the toy of my terror, my emblem of blame.

And Randall Jarrell asks in "Eighth Air Force,"

> Shall I say that man
> Is not as men have said: a wolf to man?

To be sure, that concern for the enemy is common to war poetry from *Beowulf* and Homer to the Vietnam poets. Whitman laments, "For my enemy is dead, a man divine as myself is dead." And Wilfred Owen's adversary says: "I am the enemy you killed, my friend." But the poetry of Shapiro and his contemporaries, harsh though it may be, is illumined by an underlying belief that World War II was the last war for which a rationale could be found.

Shapiro exhibits hope quite simply for a better world. While his "Troop Train" carries guns and disillusioned soldiers, he plays cards and pleads, "deal me winners, souvenirs of peace." His epitaph for a dead soldier ends: "Know that one soldier has not died in vain." Like Shapiro, Randall Jarrell, through interminable horrors, carries hope in the form of inquiry, a form of exploration. Often he asks what war's deaths are for. In "The Survivor Among Graves," the dead of "a war now, numbered / As your lives and graves are numbered" still ask: "*Say again . . . That somewhere, there is—something, something.*" And in Jarrell's "New Georgia," the cause shines out: "Who fights for his own life / Loses, loses: I have killed for my world, and am free."

The message is clear: Even in the face of destruction, many strong war poets maintained trust. They followed Auden's great declaration of 1940, "We must love one another or die." They affirmed Marianne Moore's assertion three years later:

> If these great patient dyings . . .
> can teach us how to live, these
>   dyings were not wasted.

The optimism was short-lived. Hope for an ideal world has been dashed by atrocities in Vietnam, tortures in Eastern Europe, slaughters in the Balkans, apartheid, hunger, Iraq, violation of the earth's resources, and much more.

Hope for a better world. How I wish I could write those words without shuddering for those who believed in it. Despite the bloodshed that has followed, however, Shapiro's war still resonates in art as a sudden awareness of stark horror. Though the locales may vary, though the suffering may be seen from different perspectives, though the songs are of other cultures, World War II is still ground for haunting metaphor. Gerald Stern dramatically evokes the Holocaust in "The Jew and the Rooster Are One" (1995). Robert Pinsky, in "The Unseen" (1984), writing of a visit to Krakow's death camp, observes: "We try to take in what won't be turned from in despair." Edward Hirsch marks the division between childhood innocence and the war's reality in "Paul Celan: A Grave and Mysterious Sentence" (1986), written in the voice of that German poet who survived the camps to commit suicide in free Paris:

> But what did we know then about the smoke
> That was already beginning to pulse from trains
> To char our foreheads . . .

And there are newer poets as well. One is Yerra Sugarman, a daughter of concentration camp survivors, who writes beautifully of hope and lost hope. Another, Binu A. Realuyo, in "Pantoum: The Comfort Woman," tells of a Filipina forced to submit to sexual assault for nine months in a Japanese brothel during World War II. The poem reads in part:

Rain, tell me the story once again; mine, don't pause—
sounds of belts unbuckle, dawn; blood
gorges to a rush downward.
Let me weigh their laughter one by one, past rooms of
    curtains,
where my body tilts, reaching out, upward, tied to a post
with a belt, the dawn of memory, the rush of sound:
"Tanaka—," I scream. My husband
awakens, "Who is he—Tanaka?"
My body tilts upward, reaching him, untying a dream.
Tanaka, my dear, he and the darkness are one . . .

Karl Shapiro's poems, composed more than half a century
ago, still speak urgently of "The War" and of how it would change
us utterly. So would his art. His feisty spirit, his cranky voice, his
refusal to be undone despite the guns' sharp awakening, is with
us to stay.

An Uncommon Friend

My friendship with Richard Yates began in 1961, when *Revolutionary Road* came out and elevated the classically structured novel in an era of spontaneity and open-form composition. Its seamless depictions of common people made uncommon by technical skill, the author hiding behind his creation, were at once traditional and new.

Midway through my twenties, as a staff writer for *Glamour* magazine, I reviewed books and films. One day I flipped open advance proofs of *Revolutionary Road* by Richard Yates and read its first sentence, familiar by now to hordes of readers: "The final dying sounds of their dress rehearsal left the Laurel Players with nothing to do but stand there, silent and helpless, blinking out over the footlights of an empty auditorium." I was compelled by what was not said, the silences, the adjectives alone, "final dying," "silent and helpless," and "empty" turning someone's dream of triumph into dread. That sentence compelled me to do nothing else until I read the book through, and to continue doing nothing else until I phoned for an interview and arranged to have him photographed. Dick appeared, smiling, with searching eyes, looking elegant with more taste than money: he wore a Brooks tweed jacket, Oxford shirt, gray flannel trousers, and striped tie. He walked in desert boots and carried a rumpled English trenchcoat.

The shoot over, we trudged downtown in a snowstorm and ducked into the Cedar Bar, near Washington Square. After drinks and excited talk, we crossed a sludge-laden University Place to the apartment where my husband, Jerry, and I still live.

Previously unpublished. Given as an address to the Conference of the Associated Writing Programs, February 2008.

Long story short, the three of us became inseparable and remained that way throughout the 1960s. I write this knowing that memoirs are seldom true, that words cannot capture reality. Just a few images, though: over "small steak" at the Blue Mill, Dick's favorite restaurant in the West Village, Dick would break into Army songs from World War I or radio theme songs from the 1930s ("This is your Uncle Don, / Your Uncle Don, / Hello, little friends, hello."). We hiked in Central Park with Dick and his daughters—Sharon, whom he called "bigger," and Monica, "small." Sharon and I rode bikes while Dick and Jerry loped, long-legged, Monica sitting high on Dick's shoulders, the tallest statue in the park. At the New York Aquarium in Coney Island Dick called the willowy Sharon a "sea anemone" and the impish Monica a "clownfish." Through it all the two men, tall and rangy, both what I thought F. Scott Fitzgerald should have looked like, stood together with aquiline profiles, eyes filled with young hope.

In a large way, Dick was morally incorruptible, a man who thought it costly to be harshly critical of others without their knowledge. Visiting us one evening, he picked up a glass beaker Jerry, a medical virologist, had brought from his lab. Dick turned it into a bank, and insisted we feed it dimes whenever any of us lambasted absent people. The beaker was labeled the Physicians and Authors Benefit Fund (PABF), whose proceeds would send a writer to medical school or a physician to a creative writing program. "I think that remark is finable," Dick would say, when the talk turned catty. Dick's remarks were often finable, for he did not suffer gladly the pretense and self-congratulation found everywhere in the 1960s, and for example, would call the practitioners of mutual admiration "a circle jerk." One day when a bad but prize-winning writer's name came up, Dick sprang to his feet, emptied his pockets of change, and only then let loose a stream of invective. That was the Platonic Richard Yates—the man ever trying to define what was right, and to live up to his ideals. The dark Richard we didn't know until much later.

When I quit *Glamour* to write poetry full-time, Dick's watchwords were: "Write with balls, Grace!" I objected to the gender distinction, and he amended it: "Well, write with ovaries, Grace. It's the same thing." Muscularity was prime in Dick's view: Jane

Austen was muscular, Katherine Mansfield was not. Gina Berriault was muscular, and her story in *Esquire Short Stories I* "was better than any of ours."

To be sure, I heard a different music, and served other gods. From early on, I apprenticed myself to the great poets, Shakespeare and Catullus, Hopkins, Donne, and Marianne Moore. My Crane was Hart, not Stephen. What surprised me was Dick's sensitivity to all I wanted to achieve. For poetry as well as prose, he advocated humility and hard work. Gingerly I showed him an early poem, "The Abbess of Whitby," a rondel, about Caedmon, the first English poet. His response was: "I like that sing-song. Do it again." To a later poem, "The Examination: Remembrance of Words Lost," about a failed oral exam, he listened more closely and replied: "It works the way a good short story works. Inevitability. Slowly becoming aware." (What I didn't say at the time is that his prose works for me the way a good poem works: the full meaning of it in the silences.) His silences, though, the unsaid words of this novelist's prose, came out of his belief that characters shouldn't be "knowy" but should reveal themselves obliquely, like the narrators in Ford's *A Good Soldier* and Conrad's *Heart of Darkness*. Applying this principle to poetry is rare and yet right, I believe. Though technical methods differ, as they do for every genre, both are fiction, and share criteria for good writing.

Dick spoke with fierce passion about literary standards. His true Penelope was Flaubert. He modeled *Revolutionary Road*'s April Wheeler and her tragic fall after Emma's sordid decline. He said: "Both are provincial housewives who have affairs. And both are heroines. When Emma Bovary dies, I die." Although he was a major stylist, he suspected stylists of seducing with prose, and looked beyond style to structure. *Billy Budd* was better than *Moby-Dick* because the latter sprawled. *Ulysses* ("I stretched my brain for it") was better than *Finnegans Wake*. *The Great Gatsby*, shaped into a tragic fall, was better than *Tender is the Night*. Styron's *The Long March* was tighter than *Lie Down in Darkness*. Salinger's *Catcher in the Rye* was molded to perfection, as was Crane's *The Red Badge of Courage*. Most important, he stressed the difference between sentiment and sentimentality: When Humbert Humbert sees the hair on grown-up Lolita's arms and loves her regardless—that's sentiment, that's what love *is*—being able to see the hair on the beloved's arms.

For Dick, neither prose fiction nor poetry was allowed to be "a letter home." Privacy and preciousness were unwriterly. Nor was "honesty" a virtue. As Anatole France said about the dog masturbating on your leg, "Sure it's honest, but who needs it?" Dick's argument with me at the time was my decision to go to graduate school, which would give shape to writing hours and eventually lead to a livelihood. He was to adjust ("Well, it sure beats the hell out of *Glamour Magazine*"), but at the outset he expressed fear that I'd become "just another fucking Ph.D."

Dick knew his Shakespeare and Keats, but debunked his own mastery. "Good poems get by me, but bad ones never do." On another occasion he said, "Bad poems get by me, but the good ones never do." When I noted the contradiction, he said, well, it's the same thing, but his self-defense rang with self-irony. Leaving for Hollywood, he wrote heartening letters: "Don't worry if it comes slowly at first and fails to give you pleasure, or if your brains feel scrambled, or if you spend whole days staring at the wall. You must expect to produce a certain amount of bad stuff before it starts getting good. Stay loose: don't let your high critical standards choke you up and constrict you before you start."

Sadly for Jerry and me, it was hard to remain Dick's friend over time. He was sharply divided: Sober, he was ultra-sane in his rightness, and deeply sympathetic. Afflicted with madness, he would drink steadily to ward off attacks, often violent or abusive. Correctness vanished. Rightness went awry. Once Dick visited from the Iowa Writers' Conference, Jerry away at a science meeting, and I made up the living room sofa. Late at night, I heard the screech of boards and glass. Dick was thumping a glass table, shouting curses at others, but essentially in danger to himself. Looking at my friend, I saw him both ways: uncontrolled and yet dazzling with rectitude, disordered and yet correct, elegant, true. "Mental illness is no excuse for bad behavior," I heard myself say, turning sharply to snap my ponytail in air. "Now quiet down." It worked, at least on that night.

Estrangement was foreordained, although we never stopped loving Dick Yates. Ten years after we first met, he wrote: "Knowing you both was one of the very few things that kept me sane during all those drastic, dismal years of my second bachelor-hood. I know I was an exasperating friend at times, but I can't ever thank you enough, or hope to repay you, for the unflag-ging moral support you gave me when I needed it most. Please don't ever forget that, either of you." That admission came from a noble man and a cherished friend.

UNDER DISCUSSION
Annie Finch and Marilyn Hacker, General Editors
Donald Hall, Founding Editor

Volumes in the Under Discussion series collect reviews and essays about individual poets. The series is concerned with contemporary American and English poets about whom the consensus has not yet been formed and the final vote has not been taken. Titles in the series include: